Stencilling

Stencilling

*A Practical & Inspirational
Guide to Decorative Ideas for
Interiors, Furnishings, Clothing,
Stationery & More*

Joanne Malone

 Sterling Publishing Co., Inc. New York

DEDICATION

*I dedicate this book to my father, Arch, and
my brother Ross – for their special contribution.*

Design and illustrations by Lynne Tracey
Photographs on pages 29–32, 49, 50, 71, 89–91 by Ponch Hawkes
    with styling by Elizabeth Walsh
Photographs on pages 10–12 by Bruce Postle, except Bansia by Lynne Tracey
Photographs on page 70 by Kate Callas

Library of Congress Cataloging-in-Publication Data

Malone, Joanne.
    Stencilling : a practical and inspirational guide to decorative
ideas for interiors, furnishings, clothing, stationery & more / by
Joanne Malone.
        p.   cm.
    Includes bibliographical references and indexes.
    ISBN 0-8069-0360-0
    1. Stencil work.   I. Title.
NK8654.M36   1993
745.7′3—dc20   92-38336
                                                   CIP

10   9   8   7   6   5   4   3   2   1

Published 1993 by Sterling Publishing Company, Inc.
387 Park Avenue South, New York, N.Y. 10016
Produced by Viking O'Neil
Originally published by Penguin Books Australia Ltd
© 1991 by Joanne Malone
Distributed in Canada by Sterling Publishing
℅ Canadian Manda Group, P.O. Box 920, Station U
Toronto, Ontario, Canada M8Z 5P9
Distributed in Great Britain and Europe by Cassell PLC
Villiers House, 41/47 Strand, London WC2N 5JE, England
Distributed in Australia by Capricorn Link Ltd.
P.O. Box 665, Lane Cove, NSW 2066
Manufactured in the United States of America
All rights reserved

Sterling ISBN 0-8069-0360-0

Contents

Introduction

I love stencilling! It satisfies the frustrated artist in me, is something that can be done quickly, quietly, with a minimum of fuss, and can produce wonderful results in a very short time. It is absorbing and relaxing. Cutting your own stencils allows you to drift off into another dimension. You have to concentrate on what you are doing, which doesn't leave much time for all the other distractions in your life.

The thrill of creating colours and applying them to a stencil must be akin to what the great artists of the world feel when they put the final brush strokes to their masterpiece. The first steps towards this feeling are explained in Colour, Colour, Colour where you will find some basic hints on how to create your own colour chart and just what you can achieve by using colour creatively.

Stencilling is easy and it's inexpensive! You don't need to spend vast amounts of money on extravagant equipment. How you can achieve beautiful results with stencils can be found in the chapter on Paint to Paper (or Pine or Pillowcase).

Once you have mastered the skills of stencilling, you will want to design and make your own stencils – the chapter Creating Your Own Stencils will help you avoid some of the pitfalls and make the task that little bit easier.

Stencilling offers solutions to many decorating problems. It looks equally at home in a contemporary house as in a traditional one. You can decorate walls; create your own fabrics; change tiles; add a border or design to ceilings, floors and windows; add colour to curtains, cushions, linen, bedspreads and floor rugs; stencil pictures to frame; decorate clothes for yourself, your children or to sell; brighten furniture – the list is endless.

Our homes need to be easy to live in without excessive decoration; they must reflect our personalities without being cluttered or overdone. With this in mind, the designs and ideas in this book can be done in your own home. In the chapter The Finished Article I have described the work of some of my students to show what can be achieved with little or no experience. Most of the students had never done any stencilling before going through the basic techniques outlined here! These techniques are the groundwork; once mastered they will enable you to develop your own ideas and enjoy the fun of creating something all your own.

To get you started I have included a section of stencils that you can transfer onto stencil film as they appear in the book or, using a photocopier, you can enlarge them or make them smaller to fit. Remember you can turn them upside-down, back to front and inside out or combine them with other designs. All I have provided is the pictures – the rest is your own work of art.

I hope that you will have as much fun discovering stencilling as I have in bringing them to you. Don't be scared of 'having a go'. There are not a lot of things that can go wrong and if you learn from the mistakes I have made, then the hardest part is already over.

Remember, have fun!

The Colour Wheel

The colour wheel gives you a point of reference for colour and shows primary, secondary and tertiary colours. Complementary colours are opposite one another on the wheel if you are looking for a colour to add a 'ping' to your colour scheme.

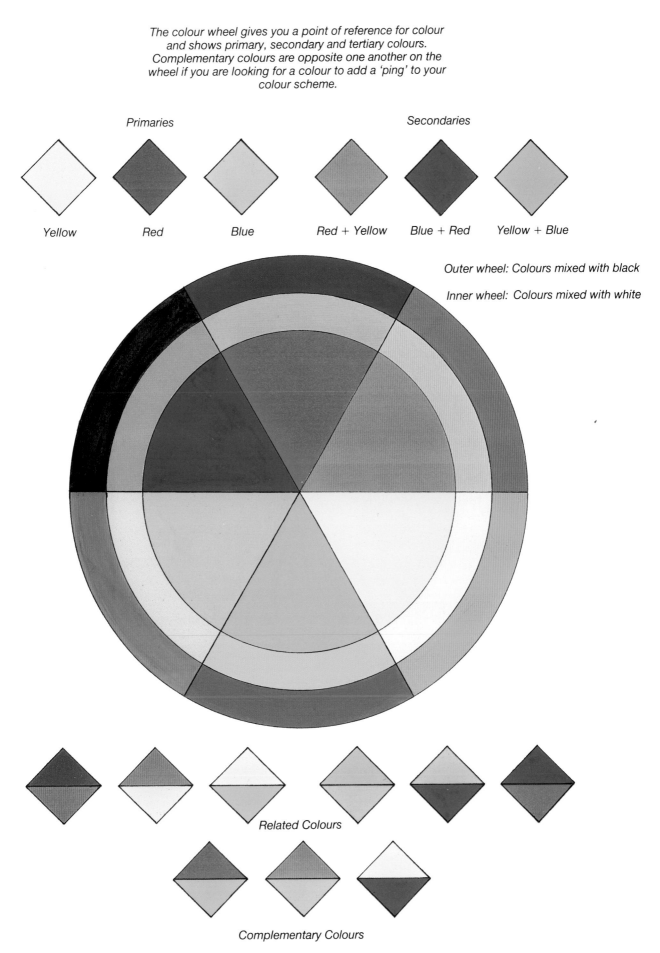

Primaries

Yellow   *Red*   *Blue*

Secondaries

Red + Yellow   *Blue + Red*   *Yellow + Blue*

Outer wheel: Colours mixed with black

Inner wheel: Colours mixed with white

Related Colours

Complementary Colours

Rose

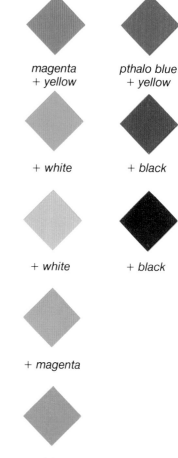

magenta + yellow

pthalo blue + yellow

+ white

+ black

+ white

+ black

+ magenta

+ black

Peer into the depths of a flower to discover the subtleties of the colours that make it appear pink or blue. Even the greens have an amazing array of shades and depth of colour if you look past the surface.

Banksia

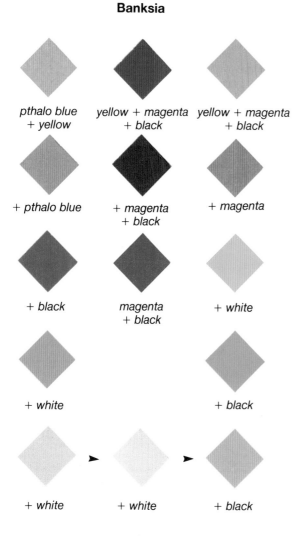

pthalo blue + yellow

yellow + magenta + black

yellow + magenta + black

+ pthalo blue

+ magenta + black

+ magenta

+ black

magenta + black

+ white

+ white

+ black

+ white

+ white

+ black

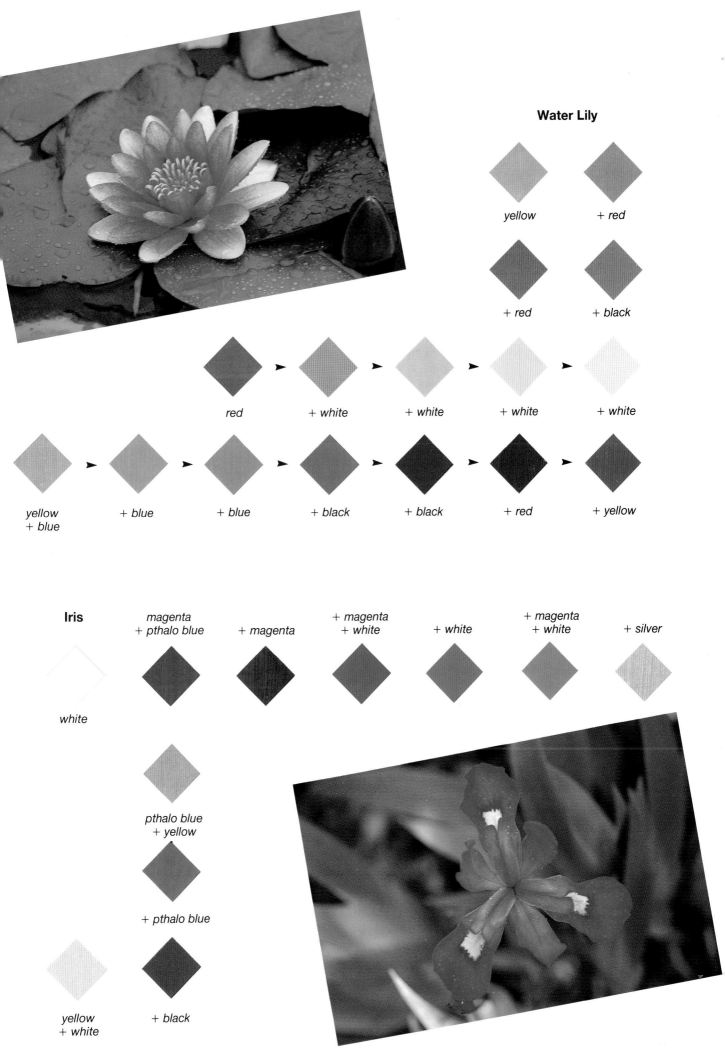

Water Lily

yellow

+ red

+ red

+ black

red → + white → + white → + white → + white

yellow + blue → + blue → + blue → + black → + black → + red → + yellow

Iris

magenta + pthalo blue

+ magenta

+ magenta + white

+ white

+ magenta + white

+ silver

white

pthalo blue + yellow

+ pthalo blue

yellow + white

+ black

Autumn: the reds and yellows of autumn leaves mellow the bright summer colours, blending them into the softer winter hues.

Summer: the bright warmth of a summer sky seems to exaggerate all the colours around you.

Winter: the soft misty greys and greens of a foggy morning envelop you. These colours used in your h_ give you a feeling of cosy security.

Spring: the sparkling colours emerging in a spring garden will give new life to your house.

The Four Seasons

Imagination, Inspiration and Ideas

Where do you get your ideas for stencilling from?

Just look around you. Look at the breathtaking beauty of a ghost gum on a foggy morning or a piece of bark or a rock. A pine cone or the pattern on a china plate with astounding twirls and textures can be translated into an abstract design to transform an old wheelbarrow or a plain white shirt into something stunning and original.

Many people I have met insist that they have no imagination, that they could never create something original. They feel they can only copy what someone else has already done. If this is how you feel, there is no need to think you are inadequate, as most art is derivative – either directly or by implication. All artists are influenced by other artists and by their environment to produce their own special style. Classical artists were influenced by those before them, and influenced those who came after them.

All ideas, however insignificant you may judge them to be, are a valid form of creativity. Whether you are painting a ceramic mould that someone else has made, knitting a sweater someone else has designed,

even baking a cake to someone else's recipe or painting a stencil from the back of this book, everything you do you stamp with your own touch of individuality, as you choose which mould to paint and what colours to paint it, you choose what colour and size to knit the jumper, and you decide to put a little more cocoa or nuts in your cake. Every time you create it is different, new, special and original, because it has never been done exactly the same way before.

Begin by looking 'in' to the things around you, rather than simply 'at' them. You will find you start to look at the most mundane things in an entirely different way.

Try opening your front door. Have you ever looked at your doorknob closely? You must have handled it a thousand times, but I bet you have never considered it as a source of artistic inspiration. Is it one of those lovely old knobs with a pattern engraved on it? Try copying the pattern onto a piece of paper to use as a stencilling design. Is it a plain, boring, nothing-of-interest knob? Put a pretty flower stencil on it to brighten it up. If you have no knob at all, try stencilling an antique knob onto the door.

Use your own creativity to adapt shapes and designs you like into stencils. Look at photographs in magazines, flowers in the garden – anything with colour and texture will give you ideas.

If you are a patchworker, the designs you use for your quilts can be modified as stencils. Copy the detail from your fabric, enlarge the design and make a stencil to match. Or why not stencil the blocks for your next quilt? Put them together and quilt around the design as you would an appliquéd quilt. Choose

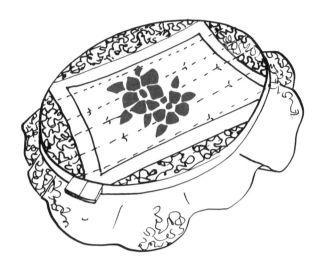

your paints to co-ordinate with the border fabrics and contrasting blocks. It will add a new dimension to your patchworking skills.

Embroiderers, stencil a piece of voile with a pretty design and enhance it with a mass of embroidery, then turn it into a lingerie bag or pillowcase. You can achieve a three-dimensional tapestry using a stencil as a base, then wool embroidery to shade and deepen the effect. This would look wonderful on a firescreen.

There are just a few ideas to get you started. Once you begin your 'voyage of discovery' you will find it hard to stop.

Colour, Colour, Colour

Everywhere we look in our world we are assailed by a profusion of colour. We are so surrounded by it in our everyday lives that sometimes we take it for granted. It is only when we want to decorate or dress that we acknowledge that colour is important. But if we take the time to look around us, we can understand the way colour interacts in our lives and how it can affect us.

We all have the ability to appreciate colour – we don't have to have a degree in design or colour theory to enjoy what nature has to offer and to make the most of it. Living as I did for some time in Canberra, where the air is clean and clear and the seasons are sharply defined, it was difficult to ignore the seasonal changes – from the harsh brightness of summer, to the mellowing yellows, golds and reds of autumn, to the soft muted greys and greens of the winter bush, and finally to the delicate of pale greens of emerging new growth in spring gardens. The colour photographs on page 12 will show you some of the colour variations that accompany the four seasons.

Colour is a very personal thing. Although there is an enormous amount of literature on colour theory, it all still boils down to what we like. Most of us have little need to know the psychology of colour or details of the relationship between different colours. We do know, however, that if a colour makes us feel good or look good, we want to have it around us in our homes and in the things we wear.

Colour is fun. Avoid colours that make you feel sad or uncomfortable, and exploit those that make you feel good. One way of making colour work for you on the days when you wake up wishing the world would go away, is to put on the brightest colour in your wardrobe (or the one that makes you feel the best). Don't choose something that will make you blend in with the scenery. Even though it may require a great effort, drag yourself off to work (or to your stencilling class). When you look good, people will comment (even though you may feel like nothing on earth inside). Once the positive feedback starts flowing in, so does the day start looking up. By the end of it, you will be on top of the world.

Not only in nature is there an explosion of colour. Look at people walking down the street. Rarely do you see exactly the same colour twice. The cars on the road, clothes people wear, shops in the street, books on shelves, gardens, even the rubbish that litters the roadside can all create some astonishing contrasts.

The same can be said for the colours you use in your home and your workplace. Surround yourself with the ones that make you feel cheerful and give you that comfortable 'at home' feeling. Try to avoid excessive use of bright colours – if you are not sure whether to add that little bit extra or not, don't. You can always add something later. Err on the side of caution; if you are working with paint it can be difficult to remove once applied.

If you don't feel confident with colours, stick with those you are sure about, the old favourites you know will fit into your life-style and tastes. As you gain more experience, you can be a little more daring and experimental. Play with colour, as I suggest further on in this chapter, and discover the fun of creating your own. If the activity makes you more aware of what surrounds you, it will be worth the effort.

Many people have difficulty in matching colours and in deciding what goes with what. Unfortunately, most of us were brought up with the concept of certain colours being mutually exclusive. You *never* put blue and green together; pink, red and orange should never be combined. Now life is a little less rigid. If it feels good, do it.

This principle allows for scepticism as you start experimenting and leaves room for exciting new discoveries as you gain confidence. Play around with some of those colours you thought would never go together and see the way they can give you wonderful new ideas.

What You Will Need to Get Started

1 Tubes of acrylic paint* (five basic colours).
2 Large sheet of white paper.
3 Pop sticks (wooden popsicle sticks) or palette knives (one for each colour and several extras for mixing).
4 Paper or china plates for mixing (the acrylic paint will wash off the china quite easily or you can throw away paper ones).
5 Two jars of water (keep one clean all the time so you don't get weird and wonderful colours from dirty paint water).
6 Paint brush – size 8 or similar will do.
7 Newspaper or an old sheet to protect your work surface from splashes.
8 Soft cloth to wipe excess water off your brush.
9 A rock, leaf, flower or piece of bark for inspiration.
10 Some soothing music to set the tone for the creative process.

*Details of the different paints to use for special projects can be found in the chapter Paint to Paper (or Pine or Pillowcase).

MIXING COLOURS

It is important to mix your colours carefully – to ensure you choose the right one for your project and to *practise on paper* before you put it on the surface you are stencilling.

Although we are surrounded by so many different shades, they can all be created using only five basic colours: *red, blue, yellow, black* and *white*. A combination of these will produce an enormous range and diversity for all your requirements. If you are on a limited budget, you need purchase only these five basics.

Rules to Remember When Mixing Your Colours

1 Red and blue mixed together make purple-ish.
2 Blue and yellow mixed together make green-ish.
3 Red and yellow mixed together make orange-ish.
It is difficult to be exact when naming mixed colours as it depends on the depth of the basic colours you start with and the proportions used – it can become very complicated but 'ish' is close enough at this stage.
4 To 'urk-off' a colour or, in other words, to create olive green, dusky pink or antique blue, add just a speck of black. Black is extremely strong and should be treated with the greatest respect.
5 Always start with the lighter colour and mix the darker colour into it – a tiny bit at a time, for example, a spot of blue into yellow for green, a spot of blue into pink for mauve, and so on.
6 If you want to mix a pale colour start with a blob of white paint and mix your darker colour in a spot at a time – be very cautious otherwise you will end up using all your white paint and still have a deep rose pink instead of powder pink.
7 To take the paint out of the pot always be sure to use a separate spatula or stick for each colour – you want the colour mixed on the palette where you can use it not in the pot.
8 Be sure to keep the lids on your paint pots, even as you work. Take as much paint as you need out of the pot or tube with a spatula, then replace the lid. Paints dry out very quickly, especially in the summer or in an airconditioned environment. It's frustrating when you come to do your next project and find all the paint has dried up. It's also an expensive habit.
9 Don't mix your media! If you are using water-based acrylic paints, don't try to mix them with oil-based paints. It sounds obvious, but sometimes we can get caught up in the passion of the moment, forget this simple rule and end up in an awful mess.

LEARNING FROM NATURE

Going back to nature (because She really does it best) is fun and a simple way to learn about colour. It requires a bit of time, five basic colours, a large sheet of paper and a particular object – a rock, a leaf, a piece of bark, or anything from the garden for that matter (the garden gnome doesn't count). Have a look at your natural object closely to see how many colours you can identify in that one item. You may surprise yourself.

If you are still convinced that a leaf is just green, look again. The veins on the leaf may be a darker green, perhaps a yellowy green or even a deep burgundy or brown. The tips will be different again. Where the bugs have been having their lunch, it may be white or a dead brown. You should be able to find at least ten colours, even if there are only slight variations. Look at the photographs on pages 10 and 11, and you will see just how many colours appear in a leaf – or a petal.

This little experiment will blow away a lot of the misconceptions we have about what goes together – you will see that in nature all colours are compatible, nothing clashes.

PLAYING THE COLOUR GAME

Now comes the fun part. Playing with paint does not end when you leave kindergarten, contrary to popular belief. Don't you long to get in there with the kids among all the finger paints and butcher's paper and have some fun instead of just having to clean up the mess? Stencilling offers you a legitimate opportunity without accusations of wallowing in a second childhood.

Using your five basic paints, on a china plate mix the colours you have found on your leaf or rock. Remember the basic rules and, as you mix a new colour on your palette, paint it onto a piece of white paper. It may take some fiddling around initially, but it is a little like learning to read, once you can look at a colour and see the basic components, it becomes easier. Not only will you delight in the diversity of these colours, but you now have a whole new palette to work with.

As you create each new colour be sure to keep a note of how it is made up, so you won't be disappointed and frustrated when you want to use that lovely orangey-red from the autumn grapevine in your next stencilling project.

Playing with colours in this way helps give a new perspective on the colours around us. Although we see them every day, we are often oblivious to how we can make use of them. While we accept that they are used in extraordinary ways in nature, we are hesitant to follow nature's lead and bring that colour sense into our homes.

The Colour Wheel

The basic colour wheel can be a very useful tool when you are learning about and experimenting with colour. I have included a wheel in the book for easy reference (see page 9). More sophisticated wheels are available from any art supply shop and you may decide one of these could be of use as you become more interested in the mysteries of colour.

The colour wheel is comprised of the three primary colours, plus secondary and tertiary colours that are produced when the primaries are combined. The wheel will help you when you are mixing – it will give you a point of comparison for your own colours.

It also helps you understand the concept of complementary colours. Colours *opposite* one another on the wheel are called *complementary*

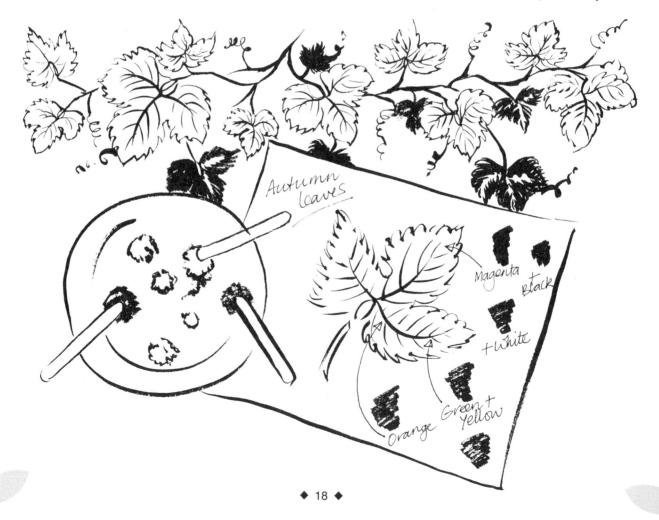

colours. When mixed together they create a grey but when used to complement one another in a design they give a 'pinging' effect. For instance, a touch of red in a basically green design, or yellow in a mainly mauve theme will provide the contrast necessary to give that finished look. This knowledge can be very useful when decorating. A blue room with blue and white accessories can look very pretty but add a little pizzazz with an apricot bow stencilled above a picture frame or onto a tablecloth. A touch of complementary colour just adds more class to any decorating theme.

The Alternative

If you don't have the time or inclination to puddle around and mix your own colours, you can always buy them ready-made. There is an enormous range of paints available on the market now. The details of the best types to use in specific situations are covered in the next chapter and if you look carefully you should be able to find the colour to suit your needs in most types of paints. Of course if you can't, you know how to solve the problem!

Paint to Paper
(or Pine or Pillowcase)

Now that you are brimming with inspiration, know exactly what you want to stencil and all the possibilities of the colours you can use, it is time to get down to the nitty-gritty of stencilling. We'll start by using pre-cut stencils that you can obtain from your local craft supplier. In the next chapter, you can see how to create your own designs and cut your own stencils. The ideas you have can be applied to just about anything you can imagine. The only difference between the various surfaces is the method of application and the paints that you can use.

PAINT, PAINT AND MORE PAINT

There is such an array of paints on the market, it is difficult to know exactly where to start. While I may recommend a particular brand or type of paint to use, before you know it someone has invented another wonder paint that will do it all for you. The best advice I can give you is to know the nature of the job you want to do and then ask for guidance at your local paint supplier. I have my favourites, the ones that are tried and true and I feel most comfortable with.

Factors to Consider When Looking for Your Paints

1 The surface to be painted.
2 The use of the article to be painted.
3 The method of application.
4 The colours you want to achieve.
5 The drying time of the paints.
6 The cost!

You may choose to use something totally different. If it works, use it.

For example: I want to stencil a wooden tray to give to Aunty Mabel for Christmas. The surface is wood, so I need a paint that is recommended for wooden surfaces. As it is a tray, things will be put on the painted surface – like plates and cups and food – so it must be scratch-proof and washable. I need to do it in a hurry (as usual, so I can catch the post) so I will use rollers to apply the paint because they are easiest to use. I want bright colours that will show up on the woodgrain surface of the tray and that will match Aunty Mabel's kitchen. The paint must be fast-drying so I can stencil several colours in quick succession and not have to wait for the paint to dry. And although I love Aunty Mabel dearly, I don't want to spend a fortune on her again this Christmas.

Because there are so many different paints on the market, there is a tendency to buy specialist paints – a paint for fabric, a different one for wood, another one for glass and yet another for pottery. While this is great for the paint manufacturers, you will end up with a cupboard full of paint and an empty pocket. There is a solution without compromising your work of art.

There are many paints that are multipurpose. They are suitable for just about all the surfaces you are likely to want to paint. The only specialist paint you may need to buy is a paint for ceramics or glass that you want to wash regularly, like drinking glasses or serving dishes.

Here are some of the different *types* of paints that are available for you to choose from.

Acrylic Paints

These are great. They wash out in water, are fast-drying, work brilliantly on paper and mix easily. They also are a good consistency for stencilling – not too *wet*.

Paints have come a long way over the last ten years from those first developed for schoolchildren's art. These basic acrylics are all you need if you want to stencil writing paper, birthday cards, wedding invitations, wrapping paper or a work of art to hang on the wall. They are not suitable for fabrics, furniture or walls. But they are very cheap, have wonderful clear colours (remember you need five only) and are a good way to start out.

New acrylic paints have now been developed to apply to most surfaces. With these you can stencil your walls, terracotta pots, paper, wood, concrete and many are even suitable for fabric (read the label). Some claim they can be applied to ceramic surfaces and glass – this may well be true, but always have a test run before you start stencilling the cathedral windows. While they may go onto a surface easily, they may also come off just as easily. If you want a permanent, wash-and-wear surface on ceramic, the best idea is to use a specific ceramic paint that needs to be fired (more about that later).

The ease of cleaning-up is a big plus for acrylic paint. There is no need for smelly chemicals to clean up after a job, and a thorough wash-out in water will clean both stencils, rollers and brushes. Any spills or mistakes respond well to a sponge and water. This saves a lot of pain when you discover you have dipped your sleeve in the red paint and dribbled, in a most un-artistic way, across the fabric of your *pièce de résistance*. A quick dash to the tap and a sponge will prevent a potential disaster.

Fabric Paint

A lot of people will advocate using a special paint for fabrics. Once again there is an enormous range on the market: ones that sparkle, ones that puff and even ones that glow in the dark. What will they think of next! There are a number of acrylic paints available that are applicable to fabric as well as everything else. They will normally need to be heat-fixed, using your iron or a tumble in the clothes dryer. Even if the instructions state that the product doesn't need to be heat-fixed, I usually do it anyway, just to be on the safe side. It could save starting all over again.

If you want a special feature on your stencil you can always use a puffy paint or a sparkling one to emphasise or enhance your design, so it is worthwhile adding a selection of these to your collection for special occasions. There are some wonderful metallic paints available that can really make a stencil on a black T-shirt something special for evening wear. Stitch on a few beads and crystals and you will be the belle of the ball.

Some special fabric paints are also very *wet*, which can cause problems with stencilling. If the paint is particularly runny take a great deal of care when using it. It may be good to use with a mouth diffuser (read on for an explanation of this one!).

Oil Paints

On the whole, these are not suitable for stencilling because they are slow to dry. However, if you are painting a wall and want to maintain the authenticity and sheen of an oil-based finish, oils can be used with additives to speed up the drying process. There is also a range of fast-drying oils available. For more information on achieving this type of finish I would recommend consulting a book on general painted finishes that provides a detailed look at this type of paint.

Ceramic Paints

As I mentioned before, the best way to paint on ceramic is to use a paint that can be fired to ensure a lasting finish. This is not always possible, especially if you are doing a window or tiles already on the wall. The solution is either to use a cold ceramic paint or an acrylic paint and take a great deal of care with the painted finish. The surface will have a tendency to scratch and therefore is not really suitable for a children's bathroom or heavy traffic areas. Care needs to be exercised when cleaning the surface – don't scrub with abrasive cleaners or a scouring pad – a regular wipe over with a soft damp cloth so as not to allow a build-up of grime on the surface will do.

Some spray paints such as car enamels may do the job on ceramics but my experience is that they can still scratch and a great deal of care is needed dealing with spray paints in a confined space. All car enamels contain lead to minimise rust and as such are *dangerous* to have around the house.

Cold ceramic paints are great because they don't need to be fired but the colours have a transparency to them that means it is difficult to work up the subtleties of shading and depth of colour that you can achieve with acrylics. They are also quite *wet*, so a great deal of care is needed when applying them. Have a cloth with some white spirit on it close by in case of dribbles. A little more patience and care is needed so they are not a good idea for your first stencilling project or you may never do any more. There is also no guarantee that the paint will stay where it is put, especially in the dishwasher.

Spray Paints

The very mention of spray paints these days causes most people to recoil in horror. *What about the ozone layer?* I heartily agree that all care and caution should be taken with our environment.

There are, however, some spray paints on the market that have acceptable propellants and, if used in a sensible and cautious way, give wonderful effects on stencils. They are very quick and easy to use and hard to give up once you have tried them.

There are some basic rules that *must* be followed when using spray paints.

1 *Always* use a good quality mask.
2 *Always* wear gloves.
3 *Always* ensure you have good ventilation.
4 *Always* have plenty of paper and masking tape to protect from *overspray*.

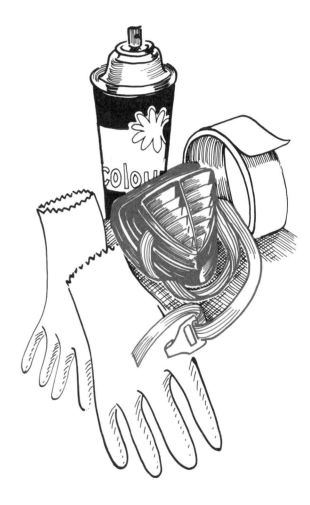

There are a number of different types of sprays you can buy.

1 Enamel sprays (take a while to dry).
2 Car enamel spray paints (these contain lead).
3 Acrylic spray paints.
4 Floral spray paints.

With all these paints, be sure to follow the manufacturer's instructions carefully, especially when it comes to cleaning the spray nozzle. They have a habit of clogging up when you have only used half a can of paint if it is not cleared properly after each job.

The sprays I like the best are *floral spray paints* that were actually developed for use on both fresh and dried flowers. I have found that they can be used on just about anything – paper, walls, fabric, wood. They come in a wide range of wonderful colours and dry instantly so you can develop some fascinating colour overlays with them. You can use them to paint a background on small projects as well as for the stencilled design. They are extremely easy to use and the nozzle doesn't clog up. The only problem is that they are not easy to find in your local craft shop. It is worth persisting though, because they are great. Your florist may be able to help you with these.

You blow through the other tube which forces the paint up the tube and sprays onto your surface. This does take a little practice but is fun. (Don't let the kids see you or they will want to join in too.) This technique looks great on fabric that will also absorb the *wetness* of the paint readily.

Environmentally Sound Spraying

The purists can always use a mouth diffuser, which gives the effect of a spray. It takes quite a lot lung capacity, but once you have mastered the technique it is a lot of fun and can give you some amazing effects, especially on fabric. It can get pretty messy so be sure to wear a painting smock and have lots of newspapers around for protection.

Mouth diffusers are available from art suppliers. They basically work on the principal of two hinged tubes, one of which is immersed in the paint. The paint must be very watery to move through the tube but still have enough pigment in it to give plenty of colour to the stencil – fiddle with some mixtures to get it right. You can mix basic acrylic paints and water, or some fabric paints are a good consistency.

THE TOOLS

Rollers

I always recommend that you start with rollers. They are cheap to buy, simple to use, easy to clean and will give you a good finish with little or no pain. For larger projects, an ordinary paint roller from a hardware shop will save a lot of time.

For small projects the little foam rollers do a great job. They are easy to control and give you scope for some wonderful surprises with unexpected colour mixes (when you accidently put the roller in the wrong colour!).

Brushes

The traditional stencilling tool is the stencil brush. Some wonderful shading and other effects can be gained using a brush, but it does take a little more expertise than the roller. Good quality brushes are also quite expensive. You can actually make your own stencil brush by buying an inexpensive, two-inch house-painting brush, and chopping off the bristles so they are hard and stubbly like the stencilling brush. You do run the risk of getting a few foreign hairs hanging around on your painted surface but it will do for a 'one-off' job.

Sponges

Natural sea sponges or kitchen sponges can create the most wonderful textures on a stencil. For instance if you are stencilling an orange or a tree trunk, sponges will give an exciting three-dimensional textured effect. Play with them and see what happens.

Alternatives

Whatever will hold paint can be used to apply it through a stencil. A piece of scrunched paper, rag or paper cloth – experiment and use your imagination to see what you can come up with. Sometimes you can discover these things quite by accident.

Maintaining Your Stencils

Your stencils can be kept in workable condition for a considerable time if you look after them. If you have put a lot of effort into cutting them, you need them to last as long as possible.

1 After you have finished painting, soak the stencil in a basin of warm soapy water to loosen the paint.

2 Lie an old, fluffy towel on a firm surface, put the stencil on top of the towel, and then with a soft scrubbing brush gently scrub the surface to remove the paint. The pile of the towel will push up between the holes in the stencil and protect the 'ties'. I wouldn't recommend you do this with stencil card as it will get a bit soggy – a wipe over with a damp cloth will do.

3 Dry the stencil thoroughly and store it flat between greaseproof paper, to separate it from other stencils.

4 When you have finished washing your stencils, drain the water off the paint left in the bottom of the basin, then throw the lumps of paint in the bin so you don't clog up your drains.

There does come a time in the life of all stencils when they can go on no longer and should be retired. I can't bear to part with my stencils and have built up quite a collection of old favourites that have seen better days.

THE FIRST STEP: STENCILLING ON PAPER

I know practice is boring, but if you want your first project to be a good one, practice first on paper.

Every minute spent in practice and preparation saves hours of fixing up mistakes and wasting time, energy and materials.

Your practice can be rewarding. Use a writing pad of recycled paper and turn it into a pretty gift for someone or thank-you notes for yourself. If a page doesn't work out, just tear it out and pretend it never existed. Nobody will know but you.

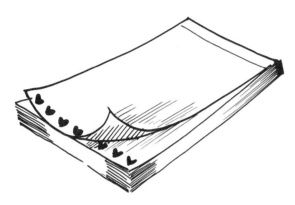

You will need the following.
1 Pop sticks (wooden popsicle sticks), spatulas or palette knives to get the paint out of the jar.
2 Rollers (one for each colour if possible).
3 Palette (a paper plate or old china one).
4 Paints (acrylic, five colours).
5 Writing pad (unlined paper).
6 Stencil (for your initial efforts, buy pre-cut stencils from a craft supplier).
7 Magic tape (removable, non-sticky adhesive tape).
8 Roll of paper towels.
9 Damp cloth.
10 Jar of water.
11 Newspaper or cloth to cover work surface.

Down to Business

1 Using a pop stick, take about a teaspoon of paint from the jar or tube and place it on your palette. It is best to use the simple colours to start, without mixing them. You can use either a separate plate for each colour or a large plate for all colours.

2 Position the stencil on the paper. This can be held in place either with a piece of magic tape on the corners or by simply holding it in place with your spare hand.

3 Load your roller with the first colour. *Do not wet the roller before you use it*. If you are using a roller after it has been washed, be sure it has been completely dried. Any moisture in the roller can make your paint too wet and cause all sorts of problems.

Wet is the biggest problem encountered by stencillers. If anyone has difficulties with stencilling it is usually related to *too much water* either on the roller or in the paint.

Roll the roller in the paint until it is completely covered, as evenly as possible. Using a pad of paper towels, roll the paint *off* the roller.

No, I am not mad.

You must take off the excess paint onto the paper towel otherwise you will have *wet* problem. But try not to be stingy when rolling the paint on – there is a temptation to put on only as much as you need. It *must* be spread evenly over the roller. If you try to save on paint you will end up with a very patchy finish.

You learn how much paint to leave on the roller with practice. Generally speaking, when the paint coming off the roller is no longer wet and shiny on the paper towel, you are ready to stencil.

4 Hold the roller loosely in your hand. Don't grip it too tightly – just enough to have control. The idea is to roll the paint lightly on to the paper. Do not press

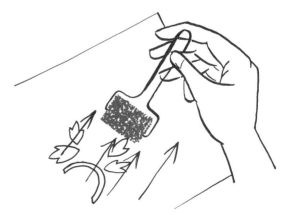

the paint through the stencil. The roller itself should not actually touch the paper. Allow the roller to do the work for you and let it move freely as it passes over the stencil. I like to use a backhand motion – your hand doesn't get as tired as it does when you are pushing the roller like a lawnmower.

Remember to hold the stencil firmly in place while you are painting. You can use magic tape to hold it still.

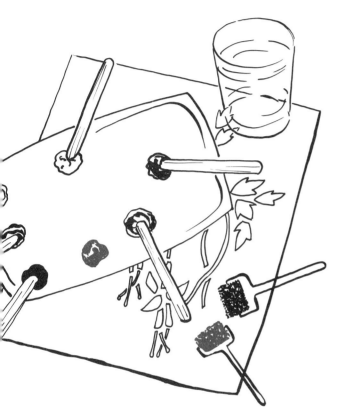

Using this technique, you can achieve a very soft and subtle effect with the paint. If you want a deeper colour, then just roll back and forward longer to build up the colour intensity. Don't be tempted to press too hard, otherwise the paint squishes under the stencil and you will have smudgy edges. Be patient – with practice you will soon get the feel of how much pressure to put on the roller.

5 If you want a shaded effect, choose a second colour and repeat the process using another roller, positioning the colour on the design to achieve a shadow. You should be able to do this immediately on top of the first colour, unless it is too *wet* and you haven't taken enough paint off your roller before attacking your stencil. And don't be tempted to look at the stencil yet – you may have trouble getting it back in the right spot again. Leave it in place until you have finished. If you must have a peek, just lift a corner so that you can replace it exactly.

You can repeat this process with several colours and achieve a very complex colour design. However, remember that you are working on paper and too much paint will look heavy. Experiment with the number of layers you can get away with.

Shading your design will give some wonderful effects – read the section that follows for detailed instructions.

Note: If you want to repeat your design in reverse, be sure the paint is perfectly dry, or clean the stencil before you turn it over to paint on the other side.

6 Take the stencil off the paper. Isn't the design wonderful? If it's not, throw the paper in the bin and start again. You can learn from the mistakes you made the first time.

7 Clean up. All the rollers, pop sticks and palette can be washed in water and used again. Be sure the rollers are completely dried out after washing them. Also, the acrylic paint left on your rollers and palette can sometimes form 'strings' when you wash them – which can block the plumbing. The best way is to use disposable paper plates as palettes and throw them away. Wash your other equipment in a bucket, strain off the dirty water and dispose of the solid residue separately.

Shading

Half the fun of stencilling is playing with the colours. You have already discovered how to mix them on your palette. Now here are some ideas on how to mix them using the stencil itself as your palette.

1 Rather than mixing together the actual paints, put the different colours onto the stencil, separately. For instance, if you want to stencil a mauve swathe of wisteria, stencil a light application of blue, then one of red, then highlight or completely lighten with a layer of white. This adds a dimension to the colour that you can't achieve on your palette and you will find that different lights will pick up varying colours in your stencil. There will always be an element of surprise. It also means that each swathe of wisteria will be individual (unless you are a genius), which gives light and movement to your stencil.

2 Similarly, shade using green. By overlaying blue and yellow in different intensities and in different orders, you will achieve lots of greens. None of these colours will clash or look ugly because they all have the same basic ingredients.

3 Try stencilling a simple flower design: a pink flower with green leaves. On your first piece of paper, completely cover the whole stencil with a light application of green, then paint the flower section with pink.

4 Use the same design again, but this time paint the whole flower and leaves in pink then the leaves in green.

5 Now mask off each section of the stencil at a time with magic tape. That is, tape over the flower and paint the stem and leaves green, then uncover the flower and mask off the stem and leaves. Paint the flower pink.

6 Next, try overlapping the colours to create some new and wonderful shadings. Don't mask off the separate sections when you paint the flower pink and the stem and leaves green. The flower with a touch of green on the tip of the petals looks far more natural. We have already seen that nothing in nature is one colour.

You will achieve a different but complementary look with each application. This variation can prevent stencil (especially a repeat design), becoming boring because none will be exactly the same.

When overlaying colour, start with the darkest colour first and highlight with the lighter colours as you go. If you put on the lightest first, it will disappear under the dark overlay. The only time this really works is if you want to mask a dark background colour. For instance if you have a navy fabric and want a specific colour in the stencil to match up with something else, stencil white first to block the background, then put the desired colour over the top of it. This prevents the dark fabric from distorting the colour.

The Magic of White

If, after all your efforts, your stencil looks heavy or lacks inspiration, use white – it is magic. A little touch of white here and there to give an impression of a reflection can give your stencil a lift and a shimmer.

Painting on paper allows you to work out all the little tricks and techniques of stencilling without costing you a lot in mistakes. Keep going until you feel confident. Play with the colour, how much pressure to put on the roller, the most comfortable way to sit or stand, the different ways of positioning the stencil, trying out new stencils you have cut to make sure the design is correct or simply to work out a colour scheme for your walls before taking the plunge.

The surface of paper is easy to paint because it is slightly absorbent. You will notice the difference when you start working on painted finishes, wood and fabric.

STENCILLING ON FABRIC

This is my favourite because I have more mobility and versatility on the working surface. The basic techniques are the same as in stencilling on paper but there are a few points to note.

You will need the following.
1 Pop sticks.
2 Rollers.
3 Paints – acrylic or special fabric paint and any special effects if required.
4 Roll of paper towels.
5 Magic tape (for masking off parts of the stencil).
6 Spray adhesive.
7 Fabric to stencil, cotton preferably.
8 Stencil.
9 Palettes.
10 Damp cloth.
11 Jar of water.
12 Iron.

▶ *The soft mauves and purples of wisteria add life to a bedroom wall. Reflected in the pillow slips it gives the room a whole new look. (Stencil pages 112–115.)*

Applying Colour to a Stencil

Be adventurous with colour – don't be afraid. Play with the proportions, as I have done in this exercise and see the different colours you can create by mixing the colours in different proportions – you will be amazed at the variations you can make with your base colours.

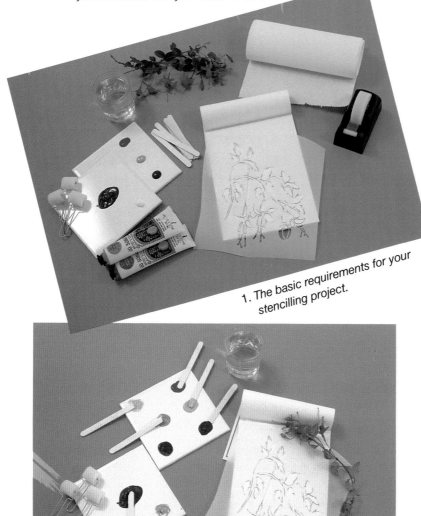

1. The basic requirements for your stencilling project.

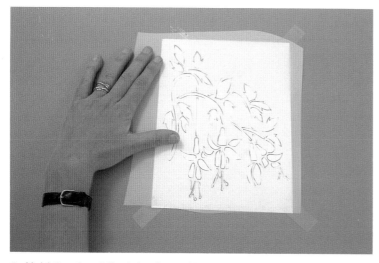

2. Mix the colours you need on your palette.

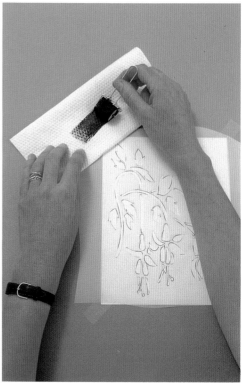

4. Completely cover the roller with paint, then roll off the excess onto a paper towel.

5. Apply the paint to the stencil with an even, light, backhand motion – don't grip it too tightly. The right amount of colour will give a nice clean edge to your stencil design. If it is a bit smudgy, you have too much paint on your roller.

3. Hold the stencil firmly in place with your spare hand or with magic tape.

6. Checking the first two layers — purple on green.

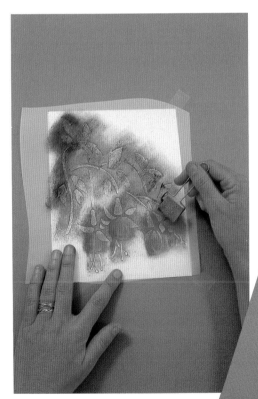

7. Applying purple on pink to flowers.

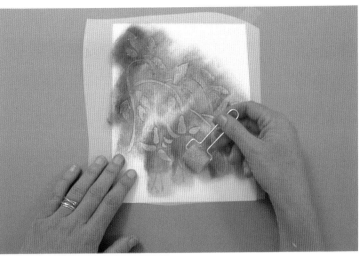

8. Applying yellow to flowers.

9. Stencil without shading.

Give depth to the flower by overlaying colours rather than using a single colour – remember the colour exercise and all the colours found in one flower? Colours can be mixed on the page by applying layers of paint directly, rather than mixing on the palette. You can vary colour intensities quite successfully this way.

10. The finished stencil with shading.

And So to Work

1   Be sure your fabric is washed and well-ironed, so that no bumps or creases will ruin your stencil.

The type of fabric you choose depends largely on what you are doing. Cottons will absorb the paint easily, while polyesters tend to leave the paint sitting on the surface. If you are stencilling on velvet or a textured fabric be aware of the pile and apply the paint in the direction of the pile.

It is far easier to stencil on a flat piece of fabric than on a readymade garment. While there are no rules against stencilling a T-shirt or skirt, if you are making the garment yourself, it is far easier to do your stencilling before you sew it together.

2   Put your paint onto the palette.

3   To position the stencil, make sure the fabric is stretched out, either pinned onto the work surface or laid out as flat as possible. If you are stencilling a readymade garment, put a piece of cardboard or something in between the layers of fabric just in case the paint seeps through. This shouldn't happen unless the roller is too *wet*.

Using the spray adhesive, shake the can well, and *lightly* spray the *back* of the stencil. Do this outside (the overspray is very sticky) and lie the stencil on some newspaper to spray it. If you try to hold the stencil in your hand, you will find that everything you touch sticks to you.

Be sure to get an all-over coverage so the stencil doesn't lift off the fabric at the wrong time. Then

carefully position the stencil on the fabric. If you happen to put it in the wrong spot it is simple to quickly lift it off the fabric and reposition it. This technique will give you an extra hand, in case you need it, and ensures that the stencil stays firmly in place throughout the painting process.

4   Cover your roller with paint as when painting onto paper.

5   Roll the paint onto the fabric, using the same technique. You will find that the texture of the fabric is different to paper. You may need to have more paint on your roller but don't assume you will until you have tried first. If the fabric is something special try out on an extra piece first. With cotton, you will find the colour blends into the fabric beautifully; silk is a bit tricky as the paints will bleed but, if you use a fabric paint and make sure the roller is very dry, you can achieve wonderful results; polyester fabrics will tend to make the paint sit on the surface, rather than absorb it. Also, be aware that the paint will build up on the surface if you use too much.

If you are painting on a darker background, don't be too subtle with your colours, because they just won't show up. If stencilling on black or navy for instance, use fairly bright colours so they will be visible against the background.

Don't rub the roller on the fabric or it will wrinkle it. If you find the roller grabs the fabric, it may be too dry. Put some more paint on to the roller.

6   When using special paints like puffy paint, use them as the final layer in your colour overlay.

7   Remove the stencil. There should be no residue left from the spray adhesive. (If there is, you may have been a little heavy-handed with it – take it easy next time.) You should have a wonderful design shimmering on your fabric.

8   Clean up all your paints and bits and pieces before you go onto the finishing stages. Wash the rollers, the pop sticks and throw away your paper palette. This will give the paint a chance to dry completely before you iron it.

9   Be sure the paint is totally dry, turn the iron up as high as the fabric will take, then iron the fabric from the *wrong* side first just to make sure it is as dry as it can be. Turn the fabric over, cover the painted surface with an old cotton handkerchief or pillowcase, and iron it again, through the cotton

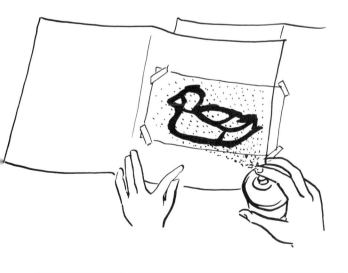

◀ *Using a single dado design, different elements of the design have been singled out to stencil the lampshade, tablecloth and cushion. You need only cut the one stencil and mask of the bits you don't need. (Stencils pages 77 and 80.)*

cover with the iron on a 'cotton' or 'hot' setting. You can also heat set the paint by putting the garment into a clothes drier. This will save ironing, especially if you are painting a number of items.

If you have puffy paint on the surface you can puff it up using a hair dryer. Don't iron the puffy surface, it will get squashed.

10 Now, if you are feeling ambitious, embroider, sew on beads or crystals, applique or decorate it to enhance the stencilled image. The possibilities are endless. Let your imagination run riot. Or you can leave it beautiful in its simplicity.

As you have learned all the tricks of the trade through plenty of practice on paper, no doubt your foray into fabric painting has been a breeze. One caution: if you are stencilling a garment, try not to put too much paint on the fabric. It can make it quite rigid and take away from the beauty of the design and the subtlety of the colours. We have all seen screen-printed fabrics that look as though they can stand up on their own. This is what we are trying to avoid.

AND NOW FOR THE PINE . . .

Painting onto a wooden surface is great fun. Simple, contemporary items can be transformed with a few stencils, while old, battered and close-to-dead pieces can be revived to their former glory with a few carefully chosen stencils. The most important consideration when painting onto wood is the condition of the surface.

Surface Preparation

Raw wood: the unpainted surface offers a lot of scope whether you paint a sanded floor or a little cheese platter. The beauty of the natural grain can be enhanced with the right choice of stencil and colours.

◆ Clean and sand the surface so it is smooth.
◆ For a permanent design you can apply the stencil straight onto the sanded surface.
◆ If you think you might change the design one day when you redecorate, put on a coat of polyurethane to seal the surface of the wood and prevent the colour seeping into the wood (on a floor, for instance). This will then need to be lightly sanded again, just to break the surface, ready for the stencil to be applied.
◆ After the stencil has been painted, several coats of polyurethane (clear varnish), need to be applied to protect the painted finish and the raw wood. The number of coats depends entirely on the use of the article. Obviously a wooden floor would need a very hard-wearing finish.

Painted wood: a stencil on a painted finish can create a work of art from a very ordinary box, door or cupboard.

◆ For an old article that has several layers of paint, the surface will need to be prepared thoroughly. Ensure the painted surface is even, and ready to stencil.
◆ Lightly sand the surface. This is necessary to roughen the surface of the paint – if you don't do it the stencil paint will just slide off, especially if you are working on a gloss enamel finish. Don't sand too vigorously or you will get back to the bare wood and have to start again.
◆ If you want an antique or painted finish, do this before applying the stencil. Later, I will discuss some ways of 'urking-off' a bright image by using spray paints, but all general background finishes must be completed before the stencilling stage.

You will need the following.
1 Pop sticks.
2 Palettes.
3 Rollers.
4 Roll of paper towels.
5 Spray adhesive.
6 Magic tape.
7 Paints.
8 Stencil.
9 Wooden tray for Aunty Mabel (or similar article to stencil).
10 Damp cloth.
11 Jar of water.

The Next Phase

1   Having prepared your surface, get ready as you would for stencilling paper or fabric. All the basic rules apply.

2   Use the spray adhesive to hold your stencil in place, especially if you are stencilling a wall or vertical surface. Another advantage of this adhesive is that you can ensure all the little fiddly bits on the stencil are quite securely stuck down to give you a crisp, clean edge to your stencil.

3   When you stencil a painted surface you will find the paint will sit on the surface, so don't pile on too much paint. This will leave the surface open to scratching and damage. An unpainted surface will absorb the paint more readily.

4   When you have finished your stencil and the paint has dried, you must protect the painted surface with a polyurethane finish. If it is in a heavy traffic area, then several coats will be needed. When the surface scratches and starts to look a bit battered, you can always give it a rub back and apply another protective coating – the stencil should still be in good condition.

STENCILLING ON METAL

There is not a lot of advice to add for this technique. All you need to remember is to prepare and prime the metal surface well. A metal primer and undercoat combined in one paint may be all you need to create

a good surface to stencil on. If the metal surface is old, like a wheelbarrow, be sure to get rid of the rust so that it doesn't eat away at all your beautiful work.

STENCILLING WITH SPRAY PAINTS

Spray paints produce the most soft and subtle shades and textures. They can create a stencilled image in a flash (or squirt). Spray paints can be used on just about anything from walls, to fabric, to terracotta or wood (they even work on leather shoes if you are feeling adventurous). There are a couple of things to be aware of. I have already mentioned the list of precautions that *must* be taken when using sprays. Now for some pointers on how to achieve the best finish.

1   *Mask the area well*. While the actual process is very quick in spray-painting, more time and effort needs to be put into preparation. The area around the stencil must be well masked off. You will be surprised just how far the overspray can reach, so be sure to have plenty of paper and masking tape on hand to cover the areas you don't want painted. This is no time to be stingy – spread it out. Once again you must be patient because although the preparation can be tedious it will be too late when you have lilac overspray on your white curtains and bedspread.

2 *Mask yourself*. I must emphasise the importance of wearing a good-quality face mask. To inhale spray paints is not only uncomfortable and distressing, it is also dangerous to your health. Industrial-quality masks are available from a hardware shop.

You must also wear gloves to protect your skin. While the paint will come off with scrubbing, you will have to wait for the unattractive bits in the creases and crevices to wear off.

3 *Stick it down*. Use a spray adhesive to keep the stencil in place while you are using spray paints. If all the ties are not secured against the surface, the fine spray will seep under the edges of the stencil and give you a fuzzy edge. The adhesive will stay sticky for quite a while and a single application will normally do for several repositionings of the stencil. If you are using it on fabric, it may need to be glued a little more often.

4 *Firm but persistent* is the best approach with the spray can. It is very tempting to be reticent with your first can of spray paint, but it responds best to good firm pressure on the nozzle. If you give it hesitant little pushes on the button, that's all that will come out – hesitant little splodges all over your stencil. A good firm squeeze on the nozzle, while keeping the can moving across the surface to be sprayed, will produce a consistent, even and controlled spray. If you have masked off the surrounds well, you shouldn't have any problems with overspray, but remember the spray is very fine, so try to confine it to the area you are working on as much as possible. Don't try to put too much on at once – allow a few seconds of drying time between sprays and you will achieve a refined finish. If you try to fill it in all at once it will get too *wet* and dribble down behind the stencil.

5 *Keep the can moving*. While you have a firm pressure on the nozzle, keep the can moving over the surface. If you point and squirt you will have an unsightly splodge in the middle of the stencil that will be difficult to disguise. When you first start out, move the can back and forth *then* press the nozzle for the spray. Co-ordination is the key word for a fine, delicate spray finish.

Using sprays in this fashion, you can build up overlays of colour that will give perspective and movement to your stencilled image. A single flat colour will look like a picture stuck to the wall, while different colours interlaced will give the image life.

'Urking-Off' with Spray Paints

This is a wonderful expression taught to me early in my craft career – it says exactly what you want it to. It means taking the bright new look off what you have created. You can turn a brand-new pine picture frame into an 'antique' for an old photograph, or a piece of white paper into a soft sepia with the waft of a spray can.

I know there is nothing like the real thing, but sometimes we have to compromise. We can certainly appreciate that wonderful rustic look.

After you have stencilled your blanket box, or your cloth mat, eliminate that just-painted look, by very lightly wafting a clear wood tone (in the floral spray) over the painted surface. Use it very sparingly, less rather than more. It only takes a light spray to add that final touch. This can be done either before or after the polyurethane finish on wood, or straight onto the stencil on any other surface.

BRUSHES

A lot of people feel more comfortable using a stencil brush rather than a roller. They feel a sense of security in the tap, tap, tap of the brush. Be sure to use good-quality brushes to avoid the stray hair getting in the way (this is inevitable if you improvise with a two-inch brush and chop off the bristles).

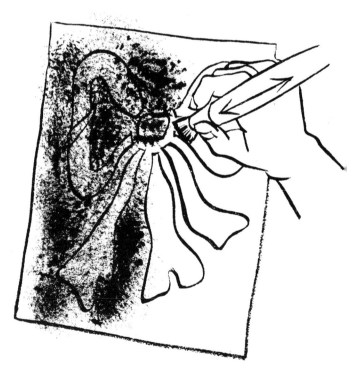

The same rules apply as for rollers – don't make it too wet. Apply the paint to the brush and then tap off the excess onto the paper towel. A wet brush will leave you with a soggy stencil.

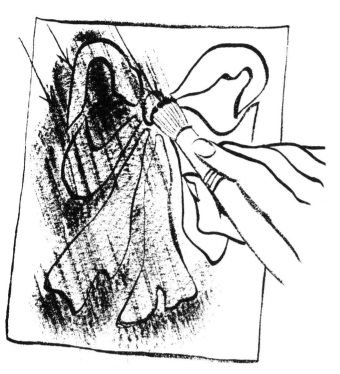

The paint may be applied by either tapping the brush up and down vertically or by stroking or painting the surface, which gives a lovely smooth finish to the stencil. Be careful not to push the brush under the edges of the stencil in your enthusiasm. By overlaying different colours with the brush, you can achieve wonderful textures and shadows.

CERAMIC OR GLASS

This is not for raw beginners! Make sure you have had plenty of practice on the easy surfaces before you launch yourself into stencilling the bathroom tiles. Because the surface is so hard and unforgiving, the paint will just sit. Too much paint will make the surface subject to scratching and scuffing, and an irresistable temptation to small children when they should be cleaning their teeth!

If using cold ceramic paints, be sure the surface is well cleaned with white spirit to remove any surface

grime or body oils – they prevent the paint from sticking to the surface. Be prepared for disappointments and be patient enough to try again if it doesn't work the first time. I tried this method out on an old milk bottle, and put in the dishwasher and it came out with the stencil perfectly intact. I then graduated to a full set of kitchen glasses, did exactly the same thing and the design completely washed off!

Because the paint is very *wet*, be sure to take off as much as possible onto the paper towel. The paint is also transparent, so unless you want to achieve a stained-glass window effect, it takes quite a few applications to build up a depth of colour. But when finished, it looks great.

This paint also plays havoc with your stencils, so be prepared to have to throw away your stencil after you have completed your project. Some pre-cut 'Mylar' stencils, however, will withstand oil-based paints.

SPONGES

These are great fun. You can use a natural sea sponge or an ordinary old kitchen-variety sponge. Cut it up into bits about two inches square. Dab it into the paint, take off the excess, then pat it onto the stencil surface. You can wipe or pat to get different textures.

Creating Your Own Stencils

Creating your own stencils is just as easy as applying paint to someone else's. You have the flexibility to make up stencils to match your existing decor, fabrics or favourite designs.

You don't have to be an artist or even to be good at drawing. All you need is a bit of imagination, an idea of what you want to make and the desire to do it.

As with painting stencils, don't expect to become an expert overnight. It does take a little practice to perfect the technique and become familiar with it, but once you have done a few you will see how much easier it becomes.

THE BASIC NECESSITIES

You will need the following.
1 Drafting film.
2 Craft knife.
3 Tracing paper.
4 2B pencil.
5 Fine black felt-tipped pen (fast-drying preferably).
6 Self-healing cutting mat (sheet of glass if mat not available).
7 A flat even surface to work on.
8 Good light.
9 Design to be transferred to stencil.
10 Metal ruler.
11 Magic tape.
12 Packaging tape.
13 Don't forget the soothing music, it helps focus the mind!

1 Drafting film

I have found from experience, that this is the most versatile material from which to cut stencils. It is thin, therefore easy to cut. It is easy to transfer designs from tracing paper (you can use either pencil or felt-tipped pen quite successfully). It is also flexible and suitable for using on curved surfaces such as terracotta pots or watering cans. It is also relatively cheap: only a couple of dollars for a sheet from which you can cut quite a number of stencils (depending on their size of course). There are some other materials available that you can use.

◆ *Acetate*. This is a comparatively rigid plastic material. It is good if you have a large area that you want to stencil. It is, also very strong and has the added advantage of being transparent. This means it is great for registering (putting the stencil back in the same place each time). It is, however, more difficult to cut and can cause some problems if you are cutting an intricate design. Because of its rigidity, it also has a disadvantage on curved surfaces.

◆ *Stencil film*. This is what is supplied most often in craft shops if you ask for something to make your stencils. However, I have found it most unsatisfactory. While it is easy to cut, is beautifully thin and, therefore, gives a lovely clean edge to your stencil, the fact that it is so soft means the slightest stress on the material will cause it to tear – very frustrating when you have spent hours cutting it in the first place. It is also opaque so it is very difficult to line up without making special registration marks.

◆ *Stencil card*. This is the traditional material used for cutting stencils, and it is basically manila board with a coating of linseed oil to make it water-resistant. It is difficult to cut, especially for an intricate design, and quite thick compared to the films or acetates, which makes it difficult to achieve a clean-cut edge to the finished stencil. Also it is not readily available in most craft outlets – unless you have a specialist stencilling supplier near you. Its lack of flexibility is also a problem.

2   Craft knife

There are many brands of craft knives on the market. They are all basically the same with some minor differences. The main criterion to take into account when choosing a knife, is that it be easy to handle and have easily changeable blades. You can buy brands that come with a pack of replacement blades.

The most expensive is not necessarily the best. A simple little craft knife will do just as well as the most sophisticated swivel head knife that can cost up to six times as much.

You must be able to change the blades on your knife quickly and easily as it is essential that the blades be kept as sharp as possible. It is a shame to spoil your whole work of art for the sake of spending a few seconds changing the blade. As soon as you feel the blade resisting against the film, it is time to change it. Dispose of the old blades very carefully – wrapped-up or in a special container – while they may not be sharp enough to cut stencil film perfectly, they can certainly give unsuspecting fingers a nasty cut.

take a couple of overlay drawings to find the one that works best. (I will go into this in greater detail further on.)

So you will need plenty of tracing paper on hand. If you are dealing with a large design, then you will need the larger individual sheets available from art suppliers.

4   Pencils

A 2B pencil is a soft pencil and it is ideal for doing your initial designs and drawings. It will also give you a dark line good enough to draw directly onto the drafting film. It allows some leeway for errors because it can be erased. *Care must be taken if using pencil on the final stencil*. It may smudge onto your painted surface, so be sure to wipe off any excess pencil marks once you have cut the stencil and before you start painting.

5   Fine black felt-tipped pen

This will give the final touch to your drawings and it is best to use for your final stencil. Be careful as you draw that the ink does not smudge. Special art pens are faster drying and will solve this problem. They will give you a finer, crisper line to cut along than the pencil and are far preferable if you are doing a particularly intricate design. They will also give you a good final drawing to transfer onto the tracing paper to use again.

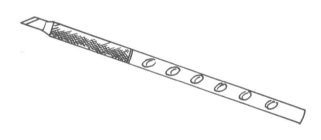

3   Tracing paper

This is available either in large individual sheets or in book form. I use it either to trace a design I want to convert into a stencil, or just as drawing paper. Because of its transparency, it is very versatile and gives you a record of your design if you ever need to use it again. Don't risk loosing a favourite design by recording it on a cut stencil only. When a stencil finally wears out, it is very difficult to copy accurately.

When creating or copying a design, I like to make several drawings in different stages. The first is the line drawing. Then, using the tracing paper overlay, I trace the design again, creating the 'bridges' necessary to turn it into a stencil. Sometimes it may

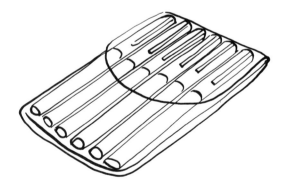

6   Self-healing cutting mat

This is a magic piece of equipment that makes life much easier for the stencil cutter. It is made from a type of rubber surface that heals itself after it has been cut by the knife, so it saves the edge of the knife from blunting quickly. While it doesn't actually keep the knife sharp, it is far better than the alternatives. Of course if you don't have access to a cutting mat, a sheet of glass or thick card will do the job, but you will have to change your blades more frequently. I would recommend that, if you intend doing some serious stencil-cutting, then a self-healing cutting mat is a good investment.

They are not cheap and will in fact be the most expensive item that you purchase in the pursuit of your art. They range upwards in size from a foot by a foot and a half, which would be adequate for most hobby stencil-cutters. The larger they are, the more expensive. There are a number of different brands on the market and be sure, when you are buying one, to emphasise that you intend cutting intricate shapes and designs on the board. Some of them are not as 'self-healing' as they profess!

7 A flat even work surface

This is most important. You will need an area where you can spread your work out, preferably one where you can leave it if necessary. I know that is a bit of a luxury in most homes these days, but if you have a workroom where you can spread out, your life will be so much easier. An old dining-room table (or new one with plenty of protective covering) will do the trick or if your family has grown out of the table-tennis craze, the old table is perfect.

8 Good light

An even natural light is preferable, so you can appreciate the colours you are working with. A colour mixed under poor light will look entirely different when exposed to the light of day. An overhead 'spotlight' on the work surface is good if you are working at night or if the room is poorly lit – borrow the kids' desk lamp while they are at school!

9 Design to be transferred to stencil

Starting should be fairly easy if you have read the chapter Imagination, Inspiration and Ideas. You will have collected a heap of ideas you just can't wait to

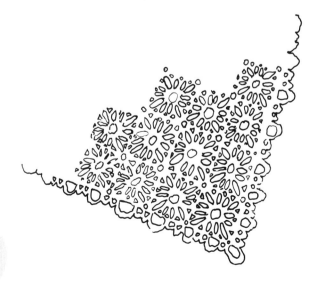

make into stencils. When choosing designs to transfer, just about anything will do – it does not have to be specifically designed for stencilling, you can adapt it. Anything that takes your eye can be converted whether it be a piece of lace, a jam jar label or a photograph.

If you have an idea in your head, draw it onto your tracing paper just as you imagine it, then using the overlay method explained later, you can convert it.

Alternatively, you can use one of the simple designs in this book. I have given a whole section of stencil designs, starting with beginner designs and building up to more difficult ones for when you have gained more experience.

10 Metal ruler

This is very handy to have by your side for drawing straight lines and also for cutting them. A wooden ruler doesn't stay straight very long after a few slips with the knife – and you can get splinters in your fingers!

11 Magic tape

This is a handy little piece of equipment that you can use in lots of situations. It is a non-sticky adhesive tape that can be used to hold things firmly, cover things up (to keep the paint off) or even for quick repair jobs. It can be easily removed without damaging what is underneath.

12 Packaging tape

This should always be kept on hand in case of emergencies. It can save your sanity, as well as repairing your stencils, and one roll will last you forever. Plastic and very strong, it is available in hardware stores or newsagencies, and is made for taping up boxes. I have found that this is the most successful type of tape to use for mending broken stencils. It is also waterproof so will survive the rigours of painting and cleaning-up.

13 Soothing music

Of course you don't have to have the music, but I find it helps block out the rest of the world and allows you to relax that little bit more and enjoy what you are doing. If the kids are at home, just turn it up a little louder and you will forget they are there.

And Now ...

Now that you are fully prepared, you can create your very own work of art.

You may have gathered by now that the actual process of cutting stencils is not difficult. *Start off with a simple design* – don't risk the disappointment of failure with an intricate one. As with anything else, practice makes perfect and the more practice you get, the better you will get and the more confident you will become at tackling the tricky designs.

Drawing and Cutting

No, you don't have to be good at drawing. Start off with one of the designs in the back of the book or convert your own picture or design as suggested already. You will find the more you do, the more confident and more daring you will become with your design ideas and in putting pencil to paper you may surprise yourself.

1 Using tracing paper and pencil, transfer the design onto the tracing paper exactly as you see it. Simplify the lines making them clear and concise. Try not to sketch as this will make the next stage more difficult. If the design you have chosen is already at this stage, ignore this bit and go to the next stage.

wrong

The bridges should actually enhance the design and accentuate the main parts, not break it up into little pieces. While in effect that is what you are doing, the final result will give a whole image, not one split-up.

When you are happy with the bridges you have created, re-affirm the lines of your drawing in black pen. They are easier to trace onto the drafting film from the tracing paper if they are drawn in black pen and you will be able to have a better idea of how it will finally look.

right

2 Take another piece of tracing paper and lay it over your previous drawing. This time, leave gaps or *bridges* between the major areas of the design. This will take a little bit of practice but soon you will see every design with bridges whether you want to or not. Try putting the bridges in a couple of different places just to see what different effects you can achieve with the same design.

3 Cut out a piece of film that will cover the design and leave enough room for the border or blank space around the design. This makes the whole process less cumbersome than having to deal with a whole sheet of film. *Don't skimp* on your border or it will make the cutting and painting of the stencil more difficult than it need be. Now overlay your drafting film on your latest drawing.

Transfer the design onto the film using the black felt pen, taking care not to smudge the ink. *If you are right-handed*, start tracing from the left of the design and work toward the right so you are not dragging your hand across your work. Obviously, *left-handers* go from right to left.

Keep your work firm so it doesn't slide about. If you are working on a cutting board, you can simply pin your design and drafting film onto the board to keep it in place; or use the non-sticky adhesive tape to keep it under control.

When you have finished the drawing, *check it carefully*. It is easier to correct any little mistakes at this stage than after you have cut it out. Nobody feels like starting again! Make sure that each little piece that is to be cut out has a beginning and an end. The easiest way to do this is to shade that parts that are going to be cut away. If you find that some details overlap into each other, create some more bridges with your pen before you attempt to cut with your knife.

4 Now you are ready to make the first cut. Before you plunge the knife into the film, make sure you have a new blade in your knife, and plenty of replacement blades on hand so you don't get caught short in the middle of cutting a stencil.

The stencil ready to cut on the self-healing cutting mat.

◆ Position the film on the cutting mat so you are sitting comfortably and are able to move the design around on the mat quite easily.

◆ Hold the knife as you would a pencil. *Don't hold it too tightly*, just firmly enough to control it – too tight and you will break the blade and end up with very sore fingers. Hold the knife so it can roll in your hand to follow all the little curves of the design.

◆ Using the *tip* of the knife, follow the lines of the design, *starting in the middle* of the design and working towards the outer lines. Don't forget to use the metal ruler as a guide for any straight lines you need to cut.

◆ Keep the blade right on the line or, if you are unsure, keep the edge of the blade on the *inside* of the drawn line. This can prevent the pain of cutting through a bridge. *If you have any tiny areas to cut out, do these first, otherwise they become difficult to cut.* Experiment on one of your later stencils just to see what happens. If the larger areas have all been cut away, you will put a strain on the bridges that have been created and they may tear.

Cut out the small pieces first, then work from the centre of the design outwards.

◆ Try to keep your knife in the film as much as possible. Each time you take the blade out of the stencil, you create a little 'edge' – only remove the blade at the corners, where you want an edge. Sometimes this is easier said than done, so don't panic if you find you keep lifting the blade out of the film. Nobody is watching you and *practice makes perfect*!

◆ As you are cutting, *pivot* the stencil so that you are always cutting towards yourself. You will find it quite simple to move the stencil as you go. This gives you greater control and prevents having to cut from an awkward or unwieldy position.

◆ When cutting a *curve or a circle*, make small cuts and, leaving the knife in the film, rotate the stencil a little at a time. This should be a very small movement to create a smooth curve. If you find you are getting a disjointed curve, you know you are making the rotations too big and the cuts too long.

When cutting curves, begin cutting the shape . . .

Do not take the knife out of the film until you have finished cutting a shape or you will produce a jagged edge.

then pivot the stencil and mat so that you are always cutting towards yourself.

Recut any jagged curves using a long, uninterrupted cut.

◆   If you find the knife is dragging or catching on the film, it is time to change the blade. Sometimes it will need changing fairly quickly especially if you are using glass or cardboard as a cutting mat. *Be sure to dispose of the blade carefully because it is still very sharp.*

◆   If you happen to cut through a bridge (and it's bound to be on the very last cut you make on the design), *don't panic!* There is a solution. Simply cut a small piece of packaging tape and tape over the cut and surrounding area on *both sides* of the stencil. Then recut the stencil. This will remain very strong and it is also waterproof, unlike other types of sticky tape or masking tape. This method can also be used if one of your favourite stencils happens to tear or starts wearing out. You can prolong its life a little bit longer.

If you pivot the stencil too sharply, you will have a jagged edge.

Any breaks in the bridges can be repaired with packaging tape and then recut.

◆   If you are making your stencil from acetate or stencil card you will find you will need to apply a bit more pressure to your knife and change the blades more often.

◆   If you find at the end of the exercise that your fingers are sore, it means you are pressing too hard. Try to relax. Let the blade do the work. If it is sharp enough you should hardly need to apply any pressure at all.

The design recut using smaller cuts and pivotting more frequently.

◆   For those of you who prefer to have different colours cut out on different stencils, follow the same rules. Simply draw your design on two or more separate pieces of film, cutting out the flower from one piece, for example, and the stem and leaves from another. When you ready to paint, do it in two or more stages rather than with the one stencil.

The Finished Stencil

Having followed all my instructions to the letter, you might still be disappointed in your first effort. *Don't be!* You can't be an expert after one attempt. Try painting the stencil onto a piece of paper and see how those little bumps and imperfections disappear. It doesn't have to be perfect to get a good result. You will find, of course, that the more you do, the quicker and better you will get.

If you are not disappointed, *congratulations!* You must be a natural-born stenciller – they do exist. You can go ahead in leaps and bounds and start the more difficult designs.

The completed stencil on the cutting mat.

You will find as you become more confident you may like to skip some of these steps in the interests of speed. I find however, that the more I try to take short cuts, the more likely I am to make mistakes. Be patient and follow the steps meticulously. It is better to spend a little extra time and effort to get a perfect finish.

SOME IMPORTANT HINTS

1 When you are cutting into corners, take care. If it is an inside corner, cross over your cuts.

When it is an outside corner, take your blade right to the peak of the corner, turn the stencil and cut down from the 'peak'.

How to cut an inside corner.

The first cut should be across the inside of the 'peak'.

Then cut the outside of the 'peak'.

The completed petal showing the neat, sharp 'peaks'.

4   If, when you have finished cutting out a section, it doesn't just fall away, *don't pull it*. It is very tempting to give it a little tug but you are more than likely to tug the whole design asunder. Be patient, and recut the edge that isn't quite free.

5   If you are particularly house-proud, I would advise against vacuuming before you start cutting stencils. Wait until after you have finished because you will have tiny little bits of drafting film all over the place. Drag out the vacuum cleaner when it is all over!

2   When cutting a long sweeping line, try to do it all in one movement. The more you stop and start the cut, the more ragged it looks. This takes a little practice and some confidence but that won't take long to build up.

3   When cutting on a self-healing mat, be sure to move your stencil around every so often so you are not cutting on the same spot all the time. It puts extra pressure on the mat and it is difficult to avoid making little nicks in the surface.

▶ *A little girl's clothes can be personalised – a pair of jeans with a flower motive adds a special touch. You can even dress-up Buttons (the teddy bear) to match. Stencils look great on purchased clothes or on those you make yourself.*

Just a few ideas you can do very quickly. Buy little boxes, towels or other gifts when they are on 'special' and you have a supply to put a stencil onto at a moment's notice. Great at Christmas time too – you can make all your gifts at one sitting. (Stencils pages 80, 82, 110, 111.)

*Dados are very versatile. These show a simple design in a
single colour, through to more complex one with four
colours and the 'white on white' effect. (Stencils pages 86 and 87.)*

The Finished Article

Many of our ideas come from things other people have done. Everyone has different experiences, backgrounds and tastes. One of the positive aspects of a craft like stencilling is the feedback of ideas. Get together with a group of friends, use this book as a guide and a variety of projects will result. You'll be amazed at the others' suggestions for finishing off your firescreen, or your own inspirations on the colours a friend could use on a terracotta pot. The appeal of most crafts is in the sharing – whether in working together, or mutual admiration, or the collective thrill of selling work at the local craft show.

I have included in this chapter some of the feedback from my students as well as my own completed projects to give you ideas on what you can achieve with your new-found skills. Along with the ideas are some pointers on how the projects were actually carried out. Most of them were done by beginners or near-beginners – just to prove it can be done.

Many of the stencils used in these projects are in the Stencils chapter, so you can do them too. The others I have mentioned are available as pre-cut stencils in craft outlets.

TERRACOTTA POTS

These are a wonderful gift idea – the paint looks stunning on the terracotta surface and they are so easy to do. Stencil a whole set of herb pots for a keen gardener, or just to give your own favourite aspidistra a special home.

You can produce an effect of simplicity with these pots. The single colour on the terracotta will not clutter the pot, nor take away from the plant that will eventually live in it. For the finished effect, see the photograph on page 71.

Hints to Remember Before Putting Paint to Pot

1   Secure the stencil to the pot with spray adhesive. It is almost impossible to hold it with one hand because of the curve of the pot. This can also cause problems getting the stencil to sit flat – you may have to paint it in sections, positioning it around the pot as you go.

If the pot is cold the adhesive may not stick to it, so if it has been outside put it near the fire to warm up before attempting to stencil it.

2   The paint is absorbed into the surface of the pot because of the porous nature of the terracotta. You may need to put more paint on your roller to achieve a clear image, especially if you want to achieve a solid single colour.

3 Choose contrasting colours to show up to best advantage on the dark red of the terracotta. When you are painting onto a dark background you can't be too subtle. You can, of course, paint the whole pot a different colour first if you want to, then stencil it. But be sure the paint is dry before you stencil.

4 If the pot is to be used outside, or have a plant in it, seal the outside surface of the pot with a polyurethane finish to protect it against the moisture and it will withstand all the rigours of the garden.

WHEELBARROW

Do you have a poor battered old wheelbarrow crying out for some tender loving care? Give it a new look.

Here's What You Do

1 The most important thing to remember with an old metal surface is the preparation. Sand it back to remove all traces of rust then paint on a rust inhibitor and an undercoat. There are acrylic paints that incorporate a primer and undercoat in one. You can paint these straight onto the metal surface. Simply follow the directions on the can.

2 The stencil can be applied straight onto the dry surface. Apply a couple of coats of polyurethane over the stencilled area to protect the design.

3 To tone down the newness of the paint, give it a spray with clear wood-tone paint to 'antique' the surface.

THE WATERING CAN

You can stencil this to match your wheelbarrow. Follow the same basic techniques for priming the metal surface.

Here's What You Do

1 The main difficulties with this project lie in dealing with the bumps and curves of the watering can. Spray paints are not satisfactory on this type of surface because it is almost impossible to make the stencil sit completely flat.

2 Stick the stencil to the watering can in stages, and stencil the design as you wrap it round the curve, painting a little bit at a time. Use a roller to apply the paint. Be sure to put a protective finish over the stencil so it doesn't scratch.

A BUNCH OF IDEAS

Living as I do, in a rented house, most of my works of art need to be removable. Faced with a blank fireplace, I decided to pretty it up with a vase of dried flowers – stencilled.

What could I put the actual design on so that I could pack it up and move it when I needed to and that I could use in some other way if I no longer had a fireplace? I chose a calico fabric. I can turn it into a cushion cover, central design for a quilt, frame it and hang it on the wall or even make a tablecloth out of it. Calico has a lovely texture and it is so versatile.

Here's What You Do

1 Measure out the area to be covered by the stencil and cut the fabric to fit. Don't forget to allow for seams. Sew around the edges of the fabric to give a tidy finish and prevent fraying.

2 Work out your design to fit the space. (Because mine was a fairly big area, I had to do the design in two stages – the vase and the arrangement – making sure they fitted together *before* I actually started cutting out the stencil.)

3 After cutting out the stencil and making sure it will fit in the spot as planned, decide on what colours to use. Stencil the design first on a sheet of paper and temporarily stick it into the designated space to make sure the colours are bright or light enough.

4 Stencil on your prepared fabric with the colours you have chosen from your practice session on paper.

5 Set the colours with the iron as you do for all fabric stencilling.

6 Fix it in place in the fireplace, either with tacks or panel pins. If you are really enterprising, you can make a frame to hold it in place.

7 Voila!

DINING-ROOM CHAIRS

Having trouble finding some fabric to match your sofa? Why not stencil it?

Here's What You Do

1 Choose your base fabric, make sure not only it is the right colour but also is strong enough to withstand the rigours of children and rowdy dinner guests. In other words, choose upholstery fabric not dressmaking. It may be more expensive initially but will wear much better.

2 Choose your design. Either copy the design of the fabric on the sofa, or, as I did, design something that will complement the sofa and match it with colours.

3 Once again, measure out your fabric, allowing plenty for turning under and fitting to the chair. (Cut a pattern out of old newspaper initially to make sure it is right.)

4 Create your design, cut it out and test on a piece of paper or an old piece of calico. The design I used here was cut as a quarter of the finished design, then repeated as required to cover the fabric. Doing it this way gives you flexibility. You can have six different arrangements on six chairs, using the one stencil.

5 Once you have completed the painting, heat-set it and fix the fabric to the chair. You can reflect the design from the fabric on the wood of the chair if you like. Once the chair is complete, spray the fabric with a soil-repellant to make it easier to clean.

EMBROIDERED STENCILLING

1 Stencil a pretty flower onto some cotton voile, then using a needle and embroidery thread, shade and enhance the design.

2 When stencilling the fabric be very spare with the paint otherwise it will be hard and stiff on the fabric when it dries and make it very difficult to sew.

3 Turn the finished piece into a lingerie bag or pillowcase cover with lavish lace and ribbon for that touch of luxury.

NECIA'S HOUSE

Simple designs and ideas give this contemporary house a touch of something special. An edging on the family-room curtains, pretty bows stencilled above paintings and a delightful rose border under the cornice in a little girl's room. The bathroom is enhanced by a border around the tiles.

STENCILLED MAT

Eyebrows tend to be raised about the practicality of cotton canvas mats in the home. Don't they get dirty? Don't they wear out? The answer is 'no'. They offer a versatile and practical alternative to rugs.

Here's What To Do

1 Choose a heavy cotton canvas, usually available from tent or camping equipment manufacturers. If you are unable to buy the heavy-duty canvas, a

cotton duck can be used with double thickness. Depending on the thickness of the canvas and the strength of your sewing machine, you can either turn the edges in and glue them or stitch a hem on the mat.

2 To make the surface durable and ready to accept the stencil, give the mat a coat of all-purpose acrylic house paint. You don't have to do this but it does give the fabric a bit of extra body. I have found that using a water-based paint on a cotton surface may cause some shrinkage of the fabric. Be aware of this and make allowances, especially if you are making the mat to fit a specific spot. You can choose to paint it a colour or use a coloured canvas to start with. Be sure the acrylic paint is well and truly dry before you start stencilling.

3 Decide what you are going to stencil on your mat, measure the design out so it will be balanced and proceed as with all your other projects.

4 When the stencilling has dried, paint both sides of the mat with several layers of matt polyurethane finish to protect it. This is the boring bit because you have to wait between layers for it to dry, then turn it over and start on the other side. For heavy-traffic areas, give the mat at least two layers. If you find that this makes it slippery, especially on a polished or tiled floor, glue some felt or non-slip pads to the underside.

5 To clean the mat, give it a scrub with warm soapy water. If you have adequate polyurethane on the mat, it will only be the surface that will be dirty and it will wash easily. If after years of scrubbing you find the surface is becoming tatty, give it a couple more coats of polyurethane. The stencils should still be in perfect order.

6 If you are looking for a bright white finish you may have a problem with some polyurethane finishes as they do tend to yellow. I don't mind this because it gives an antique look to just about anything. However, if this is a problem, use one of the newer, water-based products on the market that give a clear finish.

GIFT IDEAS

Fabric articles, photo frames, towels, and so on make wonderful gifts for Christmas, birthdays, Christenings or simply for the sake of making someone happy.

There is no need to every buy another birthday or Christmas card. Stencil a simple design onto a piece of paper, fold it in half and there you have a lovely, personal card created especially for someone special. Why not put a little stencil on the envelope as well? (Not in the right-hand top corner though.)

Kitchen gifts are always a great favourite. Stencil matching tea towels, tablecloth, serviettes, pot holders, paper-towel holders and so on. A cutlery

STENCILLED SHIRT

Choose a simple white T-shirt or cotton shirt and stencil with a simple design: a posy of flowers in the pocket, a single motif on the collar and sleeves or a swathe of flowers across the yoke at the back.

tray to put on the table at a barbecue, with stencilled director's chairs and umbrella to keep the sun at bay would make a wonderful gift for yourself.

The colour picture on page 50 shows a selection of attractive stencilled gifts.

CHRISTMAS IDEAS

Stencil all your Christmas cards, gift cards, wrapping papers as well as gifts. Stencil special Christmas tablecloths, tree skirts, wall hangings and Christmas decorations.

Stencil a Christmas wreath on your front door and smaller versions or bunches of holly on all the doors in your house. It will give you,an excuse to repaint the doors in the New Year.

When we finally applied the design to the chair covers, it looked so good we made some cushion covers to put on the inside chairs as well. You can see the finished effect on pages 69 and 70, and the stencil on page 68.

ANNIE'S LOO

Annie chose a precut stencil to apply to a ceramic cistern. She used normal acrylic paint and a roller to apply it. It looks great and the only concession is that when cleaning the area, no abrasive cleaners are used and it is wiped gently.

CAROLINE'S CUSHIONS

Caroline has lovely chairs covered with a very ornate design in her indoor entertainment area. To maintain a continuity between the covered chairs inside and the outdoor furniture, we set about extracting a simpler design from the existing fabric to stencil on a plain background for loose covers to go outside.

Because there was so much detail in the fabric we needed to pull out the focal point, a bird, and build the background up using some of the flowers in the original design. The images had to be converted for stencilling, that is we had to create bridges without breaking the design up.

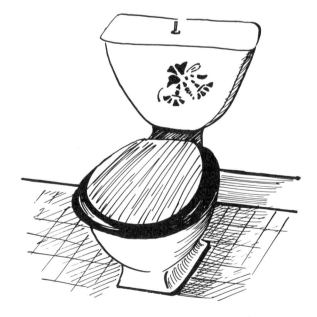

BOYS AND BIKES

Boys' rooms often miss out on stencilling in the flurry of pretty bows and flowers.

A teenage son's passion for BMX bikes inspired the stencil on page 103, which was applied very simply above the skirting board and under the cornice, leaving plenty of room for posters and other important things. The design was drawn from a photograph of a bike and simplified to make it suitable for stencilling.

WRAPPING IDEAS

You will need to plan a little bit ahead for this one. Buy your Christmas or birthday presents a day earlier than usual, box them and wrap them in plain brown paper. Use sticky tape to hold the parcel together then stencil a ribbon and bow or bunch of holly on the parcel. It is much cheaper and much more original than normal wrapping paper.

Decorated brown paper bags are great too, especially for children's birthday parties. If you are really keen you can stencil each child's name or the name of the birthday boy or girl onto the goodies bag.

STENCILLED BEDROOM WALL

Larger projects like decorating floors, walls, sizeable floor mats and hangings – basically anything that won't fit on your work table – do need more forward planning and time spent on working out what you want to do, and how you are going to achieve it.

For this project, the owner wanted a design to complement the curtains and paintings in the room and to give the impression of a bedhead. The room is not very big so the design had to be subtle enough to lift the room, not close it in. The wisteria design I used on the wall is shown on page 29, and the stencil appears on pages 112 to 115.

A bedroom wall can't be put in the cupboard if you don't like it; and after you have spent hours up a ladder painting stencils on your wall, it takes a very strong person to say, 'I'm not happy with that', paint over it all and start again. Most of us will put up with it. And it will drive you mad!

So once again, I emphasise time spent in preparation will not be wasted. Assess the design carefully.

Here's What You Do

1 If it is a frieze under the cornice on a high ceiling, the design will have to be simple and exaggerated or you will lose the detail when looking at it from a normal height.

2 Make sure you like the design. It has to be perfect. It's best to paint the stencil onto a frieze of paper and temporarily stick it to your wall for a week or so to make sure.

3 If you are a stickler for precision, measure out the area to be stencilled and work out the layout of the stencil on paper before applying it to the wall or floor. Many of us like to judge by eye, which can leave some room for error. It can also lead to some interesting improvisations to fix up mistakes so no one will notice!

4 When working on larger projects, *everything* needs to be enlarged. You need bigger rollers, sturdier stencils – acetate will last longer for lots of repeats. Spray paint is great for large areas because it covers them so quickly. Do not forget to mask the surrounds well.

5 If you are using repeated patterns, measure up carefully while still at the designing stage if you can. Measure the area to be stencilled and scale your design to fit. You can often estimate the number of repeats. It is best to start from a focal point, like the centre of a wall because that will draw the eye initially, then work towards the corner.

6 To stencil a rustic design on an outside brick wall, spray paint will be best because of the uneven surface. Don't expect a crisp even stencil – it is impossible on a textured surface – but it will look fantastic and authentic.

Sometimes even the best-laid plans go astray. In the case of the bedroom wall, after we decided to use spray paints, worked out all the colours and had everything prepared, we found that due to the slightly textured finish of the wall, the spray adhesive would not stick. Because I wanted a neat, clean-cut finish on this wall, it was essential for the stencil to be stuck flat to the surface to prevent a fuzzy edge that would not have been appropriate here. So we had to start planning again: mixing paints and using rollers. While this method does take longer to paint, remember you don't have to spend as much time masking the surrounding areas against the overspray.

Stencils

Bows are always popular

Pot of flowers

This bow would look good above a picture

Paint this design and then flip the stencil over and
paint its mirror image

For the balletomane

Stencils for Christmas

Bird and briar rose (opposite and on page 70)

Design features of the lovely fabric on the chair inspired this cushion to complement it. The design had to be simple or it would have been lost in the detail of the chair – it should enhance rather than overpower the main fabric.
(Stencil page 68)

Using the tray design as the basis, I have cut different stencils on the same theme for the cloth, dado and terracotta pot. These stencils were all cut separately to add a bit of variety. (Stencils pages 78–79.)

Sometimes it is nice to set yourself a challenge. This grevillea design is fiddly to cut, but the results are worth it. The iridescent look of the flowers is achieved by overlaying the colours.

Grevillea

Wild rose

Two more rose designs

Sprig of roses

Rose border (photograph on cover and page 32)

Basket of fruit (photograph of tray page 71)

Elements of the fruit design (photograph page 71)

A selection of rose and bow motifs

Centres have been omitted to allow for embroidery

Old-fashioned rose (photograph of embroidered quilt page 91)

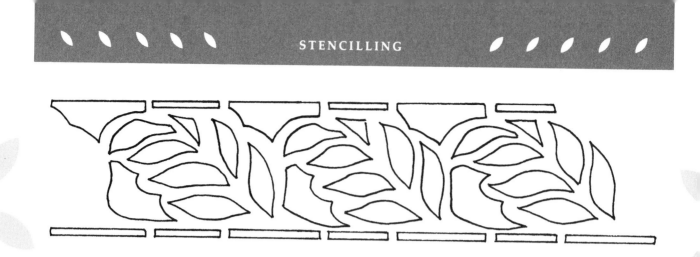

More borders – ideal for gifts

Fuchsia

Abstract bunch of flowers

Herbal border

A selection of dado and border designs (photograph of director's chair page 89, painted dados page 52)

Decorative wreath

Daisy border

You can revamp old garden furniture with a stencil or pretty up a new chair for a gift. Stencilled terracotta pots scattered through your garden add style and complement the stunning colours of nature. Keep the design simple and the colour strong. (Stencil page 87.)

For a bedroom design idea that will grow with your children and give them an appreciation of wildlife, these African animals make a great dado, cushion cover, doona cover or even to decorate school book covers. The kids will love cutting out the stencils themselves and painting their walls. Colouring books and wild life books are a good source of ideas. (Stencils pages 96, 97, 100, 101.)

Stencilling can add a new dimension to a quilt – create a design from a favourite fabric and stencil the centre section. The same design can be used to brighten up an old chair. The colours used on the chair need to be more intense because of the colour of the wood.

The stencil on page 92 has been made from four different stencils: the pot and the trunk (this page), the leaves and the butterfly (page 94). This is necessary because the size of most drafting film or acetate restricts the size of the stencil you can cut. The larger stencils are best painted with spray paints, then highlighted with a roller – don't forget to mask well around the stencil.

Stencil 2

Cumquat tree in a pot

Stencil 1

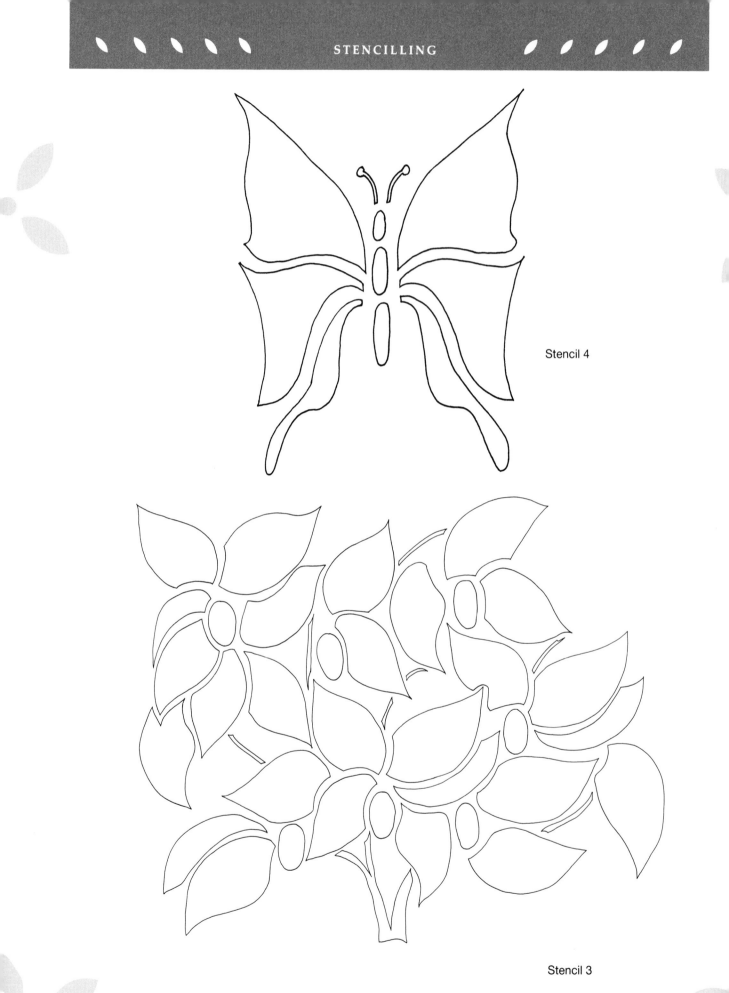

Stencil 4

Stencil 3

Butterflies

Zebras (photograph page 90)

Giraffes

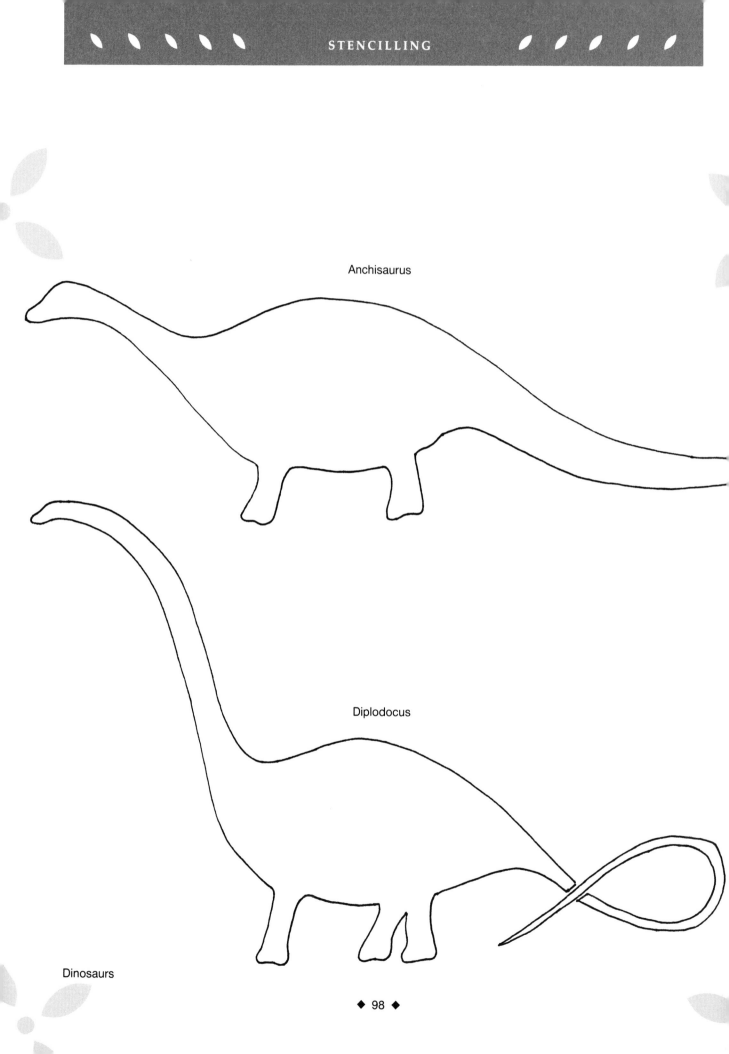

Anchisaurus

Diplodocus

Dinosaurs

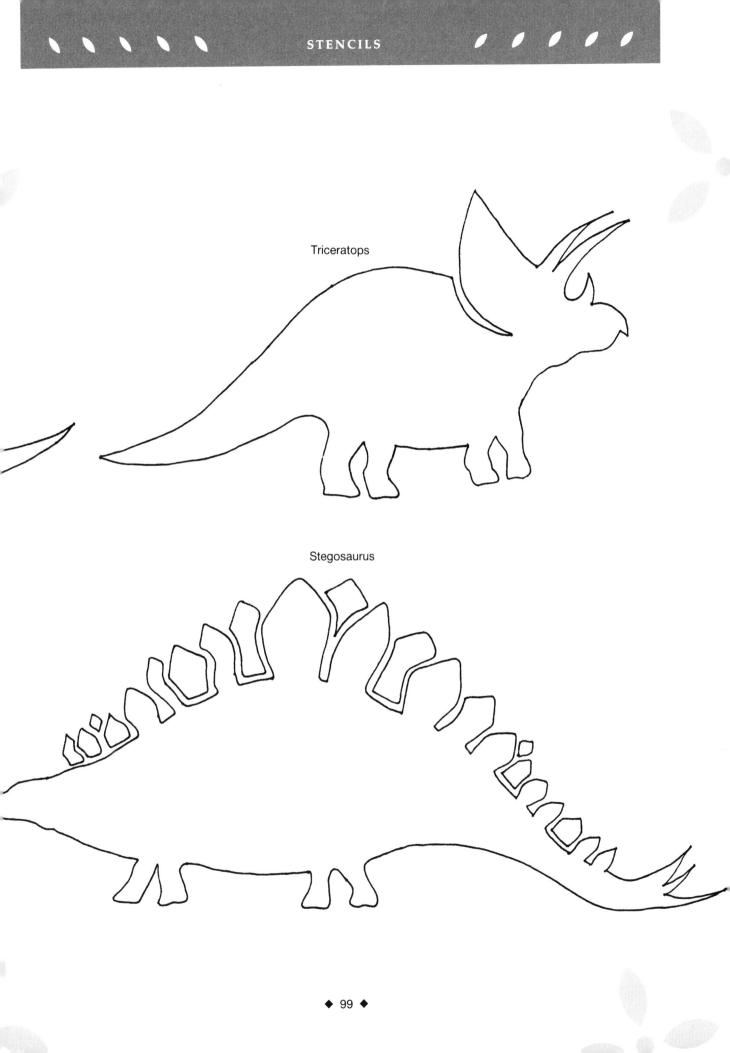

Triceratops

Stegosaurus

Elephants (photograph page 90)

Border based on a design by Dorothea M. Adams

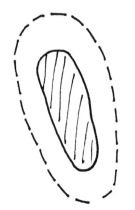

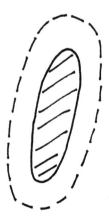

Teddy bear – the features and paws are added in with a
separate stencil once the first colour has dried

Duck

Bicycle

Orchids

Rose bud

Hanging basket of geraniums

Move the tails to suit your design

Some bows

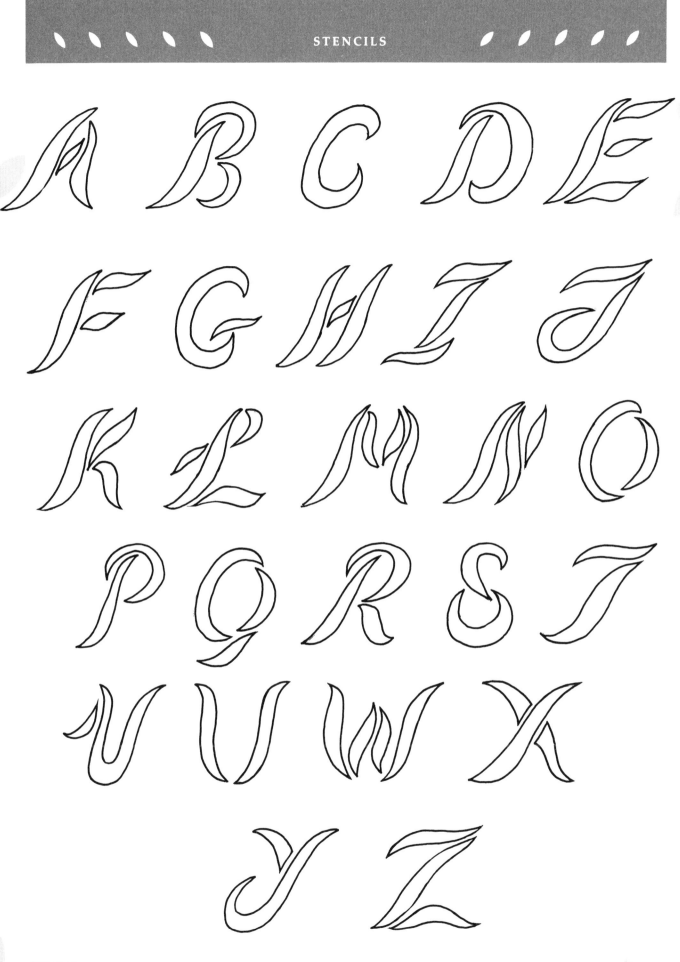

Alphabet

Christmas wreath

A selection of Christmas designs

More bows!

Motifs ideal for decorating gifts and cards (photograph page 50)

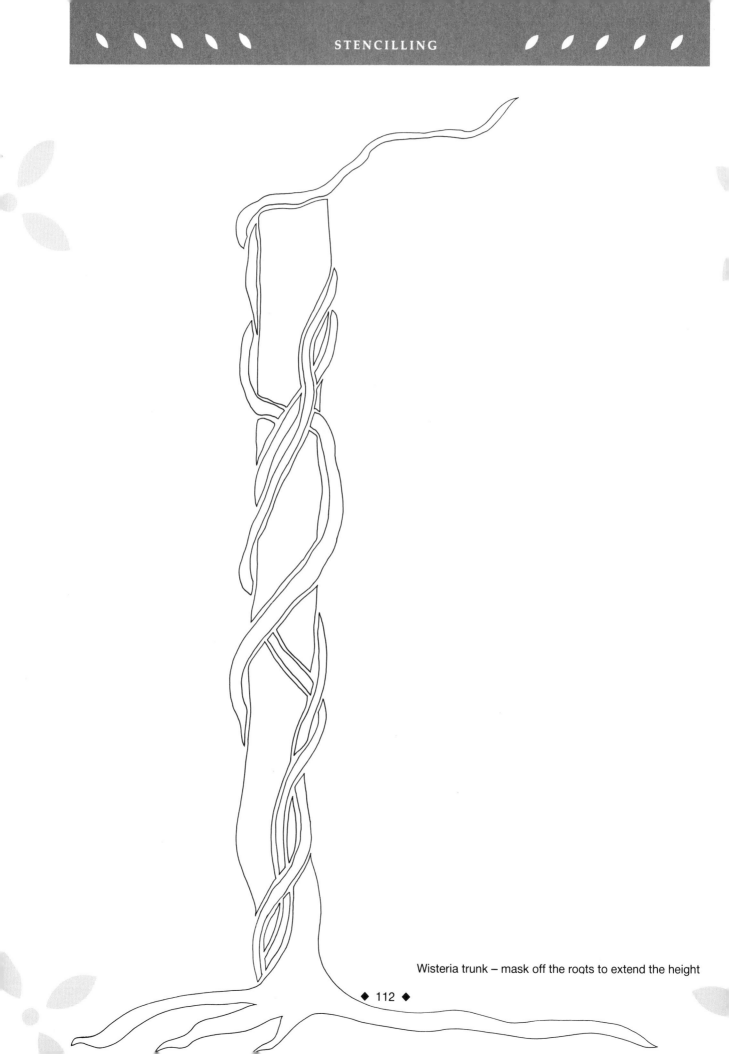

Wisteria trunk – mask off the roots to extend the height

The branches and tendrils of the wisteria (photograph of bedroom on page 29)

The leaves and flowers of the wisteria

Vase of flowers
(the vase appears on page 118)

Flower design

Dado based on a design by Dorothea M. Adams

Dado based on a design in the Trundle House, Brisbane

Two dado designs based on originals by Arthur Gilkes

Designs based on historic restorations

Tropical fish

Sunflower garland

Index

Index of Stencils